MEN
OF GOD

*becoming the
man God wants
you to be*

Men of God:
becoming the man God wants you to be
© The Good Book Company 2011

Edited by Trevor Archer and Tim Thornborough

Published in conjunction with the London Men's Convention.

The Good Book Company
Tel: 0333-123-0880
International: +44 (0) 208 942 0880
Email: admin@thegoodbook.co.uk

Websites:
UK: www.thegoodbook.co.uk
N America: www.thegoodbook.com
Australia: www.thegoodbook.com.au
New Zealand: www.thegoodbook.co.nz

the good book
COMPANY

Scripture quotations are taken from the English Standard Version (Anglicised
version) © 2002 Collins, part of Harper Collins Publishers, used by kind
permission.

ISBN: 9781907377747

Cover design by Steve Devane

Printed in the UK by CPI Mackays, Chatham ME5 8TD

CONTENTS

PREFACE

This book was first conceived as a response to misplaced thinking about how churches should encourage Christian men and help them to grow in their faith.

Facing a widespread loss of identity for men, we have been encouraged to "find our inner Tarzan" by primal screaming round a camp fire, or to delve deeply within our souls (or our DNA) to rediscover what we should truly be. This book is not primarily concerned with gender issues. Our guiding principle was to ask the question: *what does it mean for modern men to know Christ*? We are concerned to help clarify how God would have his sons live for him in our modern age.

To do this, our instinct as Christians should be to encourage each other to apply the Scriptures to the particular challenges, opportunities, relationships and responsibilities we face. This book is our humble offering to this end, and it is published in the hope that it will stimulate fresh thinking among Christian men and in those concerned for men's ministry in the local church.

The authors are all experienced Christians, but all contributions are offered by men who, above all else, know themselves to be weak, but forgiven, sinners.

The first chapter seeks to re-establish our confidence in the gospel as the driving force in the life of Christian men: to clarify the content of the gospel according to Scripture and then to explore its impact on how men should understand their identity in Christ. It is vital to understand that, without the gospel, what we do week by week in our churches, in our homes, in our leisure and in our working lives will inevitably become *man-centred* rather than *Christ-centred*. This is why we must always return again and again to the gospel as it is revealed to us in the Scriptures. Only when our lives are centred on the gospel of Christ will we be able to live for Christ.

Part Two provides briefer chapters exploring the Bible's teaching on many aspects of life that Christian men struggle with. We are convinced that "all Scripture is breathed out by God and profitable for teaching, for reproof, for correction, and for training in righteousness, that the man of God [primarily the leader, but including us all] may be competent, equipped for every good work" (2 Timothy 3 v 16-17).

The Bible therefore tells us everything we need to know from God for living as men in God's world! So each chapter begins with some biblical research before proceeding to explain principles of application, and then finally to the nuts and bolts: identifying good practical examples and case studies for the day-to-day realities we face.

There are Bible-study and discussion questions provided at the end of each of these chapters, in the hope that this section could provide the basis for study or discussion by men as they meet in twos or threes, or in a more formal men's group in a church.

Trevor Archer and Tim Thornborough
Editors

PART ONE:

Men and the gospel

WHAT'S THE DRIVING FORCE?

How the gospel shapes us

Richard Coekin

Most men get excited about cars. You think that's a caricature? I once took my son to a huge motor show in London to find several thousand men and boys utterly transfixed and drooling with desire over the open bonnets of Mustangs, Ferraris and Aston Martins.

I myself fell in love with a gleaming red Alfa Romeo 8C Competizeone, powered by an 8 cylinder 90°V engine developing 450bhp and an engine speed of 7,500 rpm. *Sensational.*

Men of all ages will watch the petrol-heads on TV trialling supercars on the roads of Monte Carlo. I love listening to them bellow with childish delight at the throaty roar of massive turbo-power even above the screech of burning rubber. Young men dream of installing a monster V8 in a tiny Ford with jacked-up suspension to launch down the freeway like a rocket.

Middle-aged men will pay a fortune to scream around a test-track for just a single hour in the legendary Bugatti Veron. There's little that gets our testosterone flowing like the torque-moment supplied by a Porsche 911. Nor so frustrating as being left for dead at traffic lights in an under-powered, cheap people-carrier. Believe me. I have one.

Most men would love to have a car engine with plenty of muscle. But it's not just cars that have engines. *Our lives all have something driving them too.* To become a Christian is to have the gospel of God installed in our hearts like a new engine to power our lives. Let me explain.

The most powerful engine in the world

This book aims to help ordinary guys live for Christ. There are wonderful chapters here from brilliant Bible-teachers, addressing the real issues we face as Christian men at home, at work and in church.

But we really must begin with the gospel of God, because the gospel is the engine that empowers everything else in a Christian man's life. When the Bible says, "the gospel ... is the power of God for the salvation of everyone who believes" (Romans 1 v 16), it doesn't mean that the gospel is God's power just to get us started on the Christian life, but then it's all up to us!

Salvation is the Bible word for the *whole process* of being brought from this world into God's new creation. It includes being both *objectively* declared acceptable to God in Christ's righteousness, and also being *subjectively* changed by the God's Spirit to become more like Christ.

The gospel remains the power of God to keep us safe and moving along the road of salvation, through sunny periods with the roof down as well as through frightening storms and icy conditions, all the way to the end. And since the gospel is the power of *Almighty God*, it truly is the most powerful engine in the world. This is because the "fuel" that powers the gospel message is the Holy Spirit of the living God himself.

You see this clearly in the dramatic changes brought by God's gospel in men's lives. Take my friend Dema for example. He was a special-forces Belarussian soldier in Afghanistan—a communist and an atheist. But when he heard God's gospel explained by an old pastor in a little Baptist church while he was on leave in

Minsk, he received God's forgiveness and was powerfully transformed. He's now a church-planting pastor in Belarus.

Or take Julian. He was a lawyer working at a firm where I once briefly worked. When I met him, he was a practising Roman Catholic, full of guilt and with no personal trust in Christ. When he eventually understood and started trusting the gospel, the joy of what God had done for him in Jesus flooded his life. When he left the law firm, I lost touch until a few years ago. I was thrilled to discover that he's been planting churches and distributing famine relief in central Africa for the last twenty years!

The gospel of God is an engine that drives men to experience wonderful blessing from God and to do amazing things for God, both now and in eternity.

However there are many other, weaker engines on offer.

Under-powered alternatives

Many Christians are tempted to try out alternative engines that drive the lives of unbelievers around us.

Some of us become driven by the engine of "success". We work all the hours God sends trying to drive fast enough to gain some respect as someone who's "made it" in life. We may be trying to become the "successful family-man" or the "successful business-man" or even the "successful church-man".

But the wheels invariably fall off when our kids fail at school, or the business fails in a recession, or we fail to cope with the stress. We can find ourselves grinding to a halt in crippling despair and sometimes depression. As we will shortly see, it is not the hope of worldly success, but only the hope generated by the gospel of the promised kingdom of God that can keep us driving through the long, stormy nights of failure and disappointment.

Some of us can become driven by the engine of "pleasure". We pursue, or fantasize about pursuing explosive sex, paradise holidays and stunning homes. We try to spit out that bitter taste of guilt that poisons every conquest and acquisition. But when our partner's infidelity or our financial problems or prostate cancer crash into us, we can find ourselves desperately alone and bitter. Alcohol only dulls the pain for short periods. We need to realise that it isn't the pursuit of pleasure but only the joy of forgiveness generated by the gospel of Christ that can set us free from our damaging and compulsive addictions to pleasure.

Others become driven by the engine of "fear". Fear of death and eternity. We may feverishly try to fulfil the demands of our chosen or inherited religious creed. This could be the intellectual denials of atheism, the eight-fold noble path of Buddhism, the five pillars of Islam, the Ten Commandments of the Torah, the seven sacraments of the Roman Catholic Church or the demanding ministries of our Reformed local church!

But there is no power in religion. It's like putting water into the fuel tank. At best it can only cover up the reality of our broken lives with a pretence of respectability. Religious observance has no power to change us deep inside. It is only the powerful reassurance of the gospel of the resurrection of Christ that can rescue a man from fear and bring him God's spiritual power to change.

So we need to start this book by getting clear about the gospel of God and its practical impact in a man's life. By-passing the gospel to get to practical issues would be like taking a car with smoke pouring out from underneath for a body re-spray.

We need to get the engine fixed before we touch the paint-work.

God's gospel is all about his Son

The word, "gospel" simply means "good news" and was used in Bible times of momentous announcements like great victories in battle. God's gospel is progressively revealed throughout the Bible as God's momentous announcement to his world about his Son. It concerns his identity (who he is) as our Lord, and his achievement (what he's done) as our Saviour.

Put simply, God's gospel says that his Son, Jesus, is our Lord and our Saviour. When we understand what this really means, our whole lives change.

Let me show you how it works from the Bible.

God's Son is our Lord

Here's a passage where the Apostle Paul outlines the Gospel of God concerning his Son for us.

> Paul, a servant of Christ Jesus, called to be an apostle, set apart for the gospel of God, which he **promised** beforehand through his prophets in the holy scriptures, concerning his Son, who was descended from David according to the flesh and was declared to be the Son of God in power according to the Spirit of holiness by his resurrection from the dead, **Jesus Christ** our **Lord**..."
>
> **Romans 1 v 1-6**

The first thing to notice is *what the gospel is not!* It is not about us, and our sin, or even about God the Father or his Holy Spirit. This is important information, but it is not the gospel. The gospel that saves is: **"concerning his Son"**. See how this gospel is

- "promised"
- "Jesus"
- "Christ"
- "our Lord".

1. God's Son is promised—
the King who would establish God's kingdom

The gospel in the Old Testament is the promise of God's kingdom, that would bring blessing to the world (Genesis 12 v 1-3). This kingdom would be established by a great divine King. The Old Testament prophets talked of how this great King would save people from all nations from God's judgment for a new life of freedom in a renewed Creation (see Isaiah 40 v 9-11, 52 v 7-10, 61 v 1-4). The followers of this King must patiently wait through suffering and persecution, until the King returns to welcome his people into his paradise kingdom.

So, the man who lives with *this* gospel driving his life will be marked by a deep contentment that is lacking in other men. People whose lives are focused on this world only will be disappointed with their wives, their children, their careers and themselves. But the man who believes the gospel of God knows that he will not expect to fully enjoy the blessings of that kingdom until Christ returns.

When he reads the wonderful Old Testament promises of a restored Jerusalem, fabulous prosperity and great personal victory, he knows that they are promises to us that will only partially materialise in the present. He knows that they will only be fully available to us in eternity, when Christ returns to make everything new. The man of God can wait, with hope in his heart.

And the man who is driven by *this gospel* can endure the disappointment of a painful illness or a frustrating sex-life or demotion at work. He will cope with bereavement, sickness or disaster, because he understands the timescale of God's kingdom.

I was once speaking at a men's convention when a man came to share with me the pain of his marriage. He quietly explained that his believing wife suffered from terrible bi-polar disorder and during her manic phases would often become sexually promiscuous. As a Christian man he had resolved to endure the indignity of her famous exploits in the small town where he lived because he was looking forward to Christ's return.

He didn't feel, as many unbelievers do, that since his time on earth is short, he should make the most of his short life and ditch the wife that brought him such pain. He explained that he was patiently waiting for eternity, when his sick wife would be healed and they would both be free to enjoy the paradise of the King.

Only the gospel of the promised kingdom can empower that kind of patience and hope while enduring such pain.

2. God's Son is Jesus—the crucified Nazarene

God's gospel declares that his Son is the man Jesus, who lived in

Nazareth and was publicly crucified by the Roman governor Pontius Pilate.

This is to say that Almighty God, the supreme Being and Creator of the universe, shrank himself down to become an ordinary man, born from Mary's womb. God did this partly to show us what he is like in the familiar categories of a man's life that were witnessed and recorded in the Gospels for us. But supremely he became an ordinary man in order to swap places with ordinary people, when he suffered the physical punishment and spiritual hell that we all deserve on the cross.

The man driven by *this gospel* understands the meaning of the most famous verse in the Bible. *"For God so loved the world that he gave..."* (John 3 v 16). The man of God truly loves God, not because he is a "spiritual person" or because it makes him a better person. He loves God, because he knows that God first loved him —and made an unimaginable sacrifice so that we could be brought into friendship with him.

3. God's Son is the Christ—the King descended from David who would reign forever

The Old Testament promises a rescuing King with all the perfected talents of many rulers. He would be a spirit-filled judge, a truthful prophet, an eternal priest, a humble King, a sacrificial servant, a glorified Son of Man—and God himself. This Christ (the word simply means *messiah* or chosen one) is seriously heroic.

I was reading recently an account of the death of Staff Sergeant Olaf Schmid, a bomb-disposal expert working with the British Army in Helmand Province, Afghanistan. This man defused countless lethal IEDs—Improvised Explosive Devices. He cleared many roads for his comrades before finally being killed in October 2009. An officer spoke of his admiration for Schmid in these moving words:

> "Staff-Sergeant Oz Schmid was simply the bravest and most coura-
> geous man I have ever met. Under relentless IED and small-arms
> attacks he stood taller than the tallest. He opened the road for the

battle group to use and 24 hours later found and disarmed 31 IEDs on another route ... Everyone adored working with him. I adored working with him ... He saved our lives time after time and he will retain a very special place in the heart of every Rifleman in our extraordinary battle group. Superlatives do not do this man justice. Better than the best of the best."

This is how a Christian man feels about Jesus our King. He is the man who laid down his life, taking the blast that we deserve, to clear the road to heaven for us. And the man driven by the gospel will admire and follow Jesus as his commander and captain through spiritual battles of every kind.

4. God's Son is Lord – the risen ruler and judge of us all

The gospel declares that Jesus of Nazareth, who lived and died and rose again in Israel 2000 years ago—is the Lord of all. One day every eye will see him, and know that this is true. Every knee will bow to Jesus when he returns to judge the world.

And on that day, those who have come to Jesus and accepted his lordship over them will bow with tears of joy and gratitude. But those who have rejected Jesus in this world will bow before him in terror, knowing that those who have denied him will face his wrath as judge on the last day.

So the man of God who knows that Jesus is our judge will care most *about pleasing him*. He will live for the commendations and medals that our Lord will award to his men on Judgment Day more than for the temporary awards of this passing world. He will strive to be worthy of the words of Jesus as he welcomes us home saying, "Well done, good and faithful servant". The tone of his voice and the smile on his face will fill our hearts with warmth through the millenia of eternal life.

So the gospel proclaims that God's Son is the promised King—Jesus Christ is our Lord. That is who he is.

But it also proclaims *what he has done*—that he is our Saviour.

God's Son is our Saviour!

Again there are four parts to the Gospel's proclamation of Christ achievement as our Saviour.

- He came as our King
- died for our sins
- rose to be our ruler
- and will return to judge.

Each of these gospel facts profoundly shapes the life of a man of God.

1. Christ came as our King—
so we gladly submit to his rule

> The beginning of the gospel about Jesus Christ, the Son of God ... Jesus went into Galilee proclaiming the gospel of God. "The time has come", he said. "The kingdom of God is near. Repent and believe the gospel" **Mark 1 v 1, 14-15**

The Gospels tell us that King Jesus demonstrated his style of government with public and private displays of incredibly gracious forgiveness, wise teaching and stunning miracles. He showed himself to be King over all creation.

The man who has *this gospel* driving his life will let Jesus' priorities steer his life. We may admire sportsmen, celebrities, business leaders and politicians, but we will want to follow Jesus. Christ came to be our King and we delight to be his subjects.

I recently went to the Millenium Stadium in Cardiff, Wales, to watch the titanic opening clash of the Six Nations Rugby Tournament between England and Wales. As we approached the famous stadium, caught up in a noisy torrent of 75,000 excited fans, I was humbled to see in the middle of the crowd, a young man calling to the passing crowds over a loud-hailer.

He was young and fashionably dressed. But as I drew nearer, I heard him crying out to the crowds with great passion the truths of the gospel. Whether or not his tactics were effective, here was someone who had been empowered by God's gospel, and was willing to stand up for Jesus before a vast and cynical crowd. The gospel of Christ his King gave him real courage.

2. Christ died for our sins—
we are pardoned for all our crimes

> By this gospel you are saved, if you hold firmly to the word I preached to you. Otherwise, you have believed in vain. For what I received I passed on to you as of first importance: that Christ died for our sins according to the Scriptures, that he was buried..."
>
> **1 Corinthians 15 v 1-4**

Notice some important things about Jesus' death.

- **"Christ died for our sins"**—this means that Christ died voluntarily (not as an unwilling victim) for our sins—as our substitute.

- **"according to the Scriptures"** means that Jesus died as the Old testament explains it. For example, in Exodus 12, as our Passover sacrifice to avert God's wrath. Or in Leviticus 16, as our atonement sacrifice to satisfy God and so permit us to live in God's presence.

- **"he was buried"** is the proof that Jesus really died. Despite what some teach, the Lord Jesus did not swoon after his torturous beatings and horrific, public crucifixion, and then just revive after three days in the tomb without medical care to spring out of his burial cloths, kick down the stone door, overpower the Roman guards and run into Jerusalem to convince his stupid disciples that he was alive again! Jesus' body was confirmed dead by the execution squad and the Roman governor and then released to his friends who buried him.

The man who knows this gospel isn't terrified of God anymore. The man who knows these truths rejoices that Jesus loves him deeply, because he died for him; he approaches God boldly in prayer because he knows that Jesus was "pierced for our transgressions" to bring us to God; and the man who knows this faces his own death in the confidence of heaven.

Men who understand this gospel also know that Jesus' death is not a theory or fantasy but a solid historical fact.

And they know that at the heart of this gospel is a simple *swap*. Christ became an ordinary man like us. He did this so that he could be treated like us on the cross, so we can be treated like him —and accepted as sons in God's family. Men who know this can simply say: "He died in my place". They love their Saviour, and will do absolutely *anything* for him.

3. Christ rose to reign supreme forever— we are alive through him today

> He was raised on the third day according to the Scripture, and ...
> he appeared to Peter, and then to the Twelve...
>
> **1 Corinthians 15 v 4-5**

Jesus was raised—not just resuscitated only to die again when he was older. Nor was his spirit lifted up in a cycle of reincarnations. This was *his body* transformed for eternal life.

The resurrection of Christ shows that he is the appointed judge of all, that he has finished paying for our sins on the cross and that in union with him we have been accepted by God. He can empower us with his resurrection life if we are plugged into him by faith.

Paul reminds us that this victorious resurrection was undeniable because "he appeared" to many people.

The man who believes *this gospel* will answer the doubts of his own heart and of others with the sensible evidence for the resurrection of Christ. And the man of God will pray for his family and friends to come to Christ, in order to bury them (or be buried by them) in the sure hope of seeing them again in eternity.

4. Christ will return to judge— so we try to please him and warn unbelievers

> This will take place on the day when God will judge men's secrets through Jesus Christ, as my gospel declares.　　**Romans 2 v 16**

Many Christians are unaware that the coming day of judgment is explicitly said in the Bible to be an integral part of the gospel.

Christ's judgment will plainly involve sentencing unrepentant people to the eternal torments of life without God. Jesus constantly warned that this will be more horrible than we could possibly imagine—like burning alive in flames or being infested with worms or rotting alone in darkness. This is not because God is cruel, but because all the goodness of God that we enjoy even in this world is gone if we are excluded from His presence.

Wonderfully, God has done *everything* necessary for sinners to join him in eternity at the immeasurable cost of sacrificing his own Son. When Christ returns, he will renew creation by his resurrection power as a glorious garden-city where countless people from all nations will party with Christ forever.

The man of God with this gospel driving his life will be praying for any opportunities to speak to his family and friends about the Saviour.

God's gospel proclaims that his Son is our Saviour—who came as our King, died for our sins, rose to rule and will return to judge.

God's "V8 gospel" proclaims that Jesus is our Lord and our Saviour. This is the engine that brings a man more thrilling blessings than a thousand Ferraris and Lamborghinis.

The benefits of the gospel are the joys of life in God's kingdom

God's gospel is described in the Bible in a huge variety of ways. It is the gospel of grace, peace, hope, life and righteousness, because these are the glorious benefits that the gospel brings to anyone who believes it.

When we come to Jesus, we daily experience, even in the middle of tragedy and pain, the kindness of his grace every day, the reassurance of peace with God, the encouragement of our hope of being with him in heaven, and a deeply satisfying fullness of life in personal relationship with him in his righteousness. These blessings of the gospel amount to the life in the kingdom of God that was promised to Abraham. The man with this gospel as the engine of his life is filled with inexpressible joy.

To summarise, God's gospel declares that his Son is our Lord and our Saviour—who came as King, died for our sins, rose to rule and will return to judge. Through him we begin to enjoy the delights of God's eternal Kingdom. This is the most powerful engine in all the world. This engine has driven men to do extraordinary things for Jesus.

Andrew Fisher is the racing driver famous throughout Australia for his V8 Ute, which is named and painted "Jesus". I asked him how he got to name his car "Jesus".

He explained that he had gone home from a men's convention fired up to serve Jesus and told his wife that he wanted to make Jesus famous. "Of course, if you really meant that," she replied, "you'd paint the name Jesus all over your car!"

Don't you just love it when your wife brings you down to earth?

So he did what she challenged him to do. And now the "Jesus. It's all about life" campaign is making Jesus famous throughout Australia. There is a man who did something bold for Jesus because God's gospel was installed as the engine of his life. What could you do as the man you are, in your circumstances? What could the engine of God's gospel , fuelled by his Spirit, drive you to do for him?

Read the rest of this book for some practical suggestions!

DISCUSS

Q1. "What's the driving force?" Think about what motivates you as a person. What might people say who know you? What parts of your life are not currently driven by the gospel?

Q2. What was it that first attracted you to Christ? How has your understanding of the gospel developed since then?

Q3. How should the lordship of Christ affect the way you make decisions and plans?

Q4. How should the events of Christ's life change the priorities you have for yourself and your family?

Q5. Which parts of the gospel as described in this chapter are you most shaky on understanding or believing? What can you do about that?

2 · WHAT IT MEANS TO BE GOD'S MAN

Men of God

Phillip Jensen

New Man? Macho Man? Career Man? There are many competing calls from our culture for men. But what does it mean to be a Man of God? At the opening of the 21st century there is great confusion in the western world as to what it means to be a man. The world's understanding is in direct opposition to the Bible's view. A world which excludes God can only define "man" in terms of "biological man", "sensual man" or "economic man", an incredibly narrow outlook, which, in practice, means that man can never rise above himself. The secular philosopher Alexander Pope wrote: "The proper study of mankind is man", an entirely logical conclusion for the humanist in the absence of a Personal and Creator God—but one full of futility and ultimately utterly devoid of hope.

Conversely, it is this same Creator God who defines what it means for man to be a man. The Bible describes man in relational terms: creature and Creator, husband and wife, father and son, citizen and neighbour. Man's fundamental relationship is to be with God the Creator, through whom all other relationships find their place and meaning. It is only in this relationship that the Christian man has with God through Christ that we really understand what it means to be a man. Therefore, the proper study of mankind is not mankind but Jesus, the man of God.

But what does it mean to be a "man of God"? The phrase occurs 80 times in the Bible. The "man of God" in the Old Testament was God's appointed leader to execute God's works as God's agent eg: Moses, David. There was often a militaristic undertone to the calling and task. In the New Testament, on the only two occasions the phrase is used, Paul highlights this "warrior" theme to Timothy. (**1 Timothy 6 v 11-12**: "you man of God ... fight the good fight" and **2 Timothy 3 v 17**: "that the man of God may be competent, equipped for every good work".) Thus in Bible thinking, in gospel terms, the "man of God" is a warrior engaged in a war.

Hymns of an earlier generation reflected this biblical imagery—"Soldiers of Christ arise" and "Fight the good fight". Today, we tend to downplay the fact that in the Old Testament God is known as the "God of Hosts", that the judges and kings of Israel were called to subdue nations and that the Messiah would dash to pieces the princes of nations! Along with this, we have also tended to lose sight of the warfare to which the "man of God", the Christian, is called today—namely one of spiritual warfare **(Ephesians 6)**.

The Christian man is not called upon to fight other men for the cause of Christ but rather, to fight against the spiritual enemies of God—"the principalities and powers".

To battle against not the symptoms of man's problems but the disease itself that is destroying the world, namely sin.

In order to wage this warfare, Christian men are called to put on the full armour of God—truth and righteousness, the gospel of peace and faith, the word of God and prayer. (Ephesians 6). The Christian warrior is not to be armed with the weapons of this world but with spiritual weaponry necessary for the spiritual battle. The "man of God" will need courage and perseverance, tenacity and patience to fight this fight. It is of course the calling of every Christian, but particularly of Christian men. We are to fight in three ways using the three weapons at our disposal: prayer, holiness and the Scriptures.

1. Prayer

"I desire then that in every place the men should pray, lifting holy hands without anger or quarrelling." **1 Timothy 2 v 8**

This is primarily how men are to act and fight. The emphasis is on praying. The important thing is not posture but purity, not the "lifting" but the "holiness" of the hands! In context, Paul is addressing how men and women are to behave in church. He is making the point that prayer is primarily the responsibility of the men. Men are to be prayerful; this is one of the chief ways men are to fight the good fight.

The temptation for men in the home is to want to rule without taking responsibility, and in the church to seek the submission of others rather than serving others. The natural tendency is to seek to impose or enforce by dint of natural power and strength. Christian men are to be strong and they are to be good fighters, yet not with violent, domineering hands, but prayerful, peaceful hands—"lifting holy hands without anger or quarrelling". Taking the lead in prayer in both the family of God and their own families is where the battle is to be joined.

Faced with conflicts in life at home, in the church, at business, in relationships, for the gospel—our first duty is to pray! It is the hardest thing to do, not least because it a battle, a spiritual war. It humbles us, it reminds us of our utter dependence as men upon God alone. But mighty works of God take place when his warriors pray—just remember Elijah, "a man with a nature like ours" **(James 5 v 17).**

2. Holiness

"As for you, O man of God, flee these things. Pursue righteousness, godliness, faith, love, steadfastness, gentleness. Fight the good fight of the faith." **1 Timothy 6 v 11-12**

Again, the context is important. It is about the relationship and choice between "godliness" and "gain". Corrupt teachers saw "godliness" as a means to financial, material "gain". Such teachers and teaching are never far away from the church, as is seen today in the so-called "health, wealth and happiness gospel". Such teaching is a far cry from the Son of God, who had nowhere to lay his head.

Godliness is not to be used as a means to financial gain since "the love of money is a root of all kinds of evils" (1 Timothy 6 v 10). Rather, the man of God is called to fight a two-stage strategy—to simultaneously flee and pursue, to shun and embrace, to take off our filthy rags and put on Christ's righteousness.

Flee, shun, put off, run away from materialism, from sin, from all manner of evil. Don't give it a home, don't nurture it, don't offer it a foothold. Be ruthless. "You cannot serve God and Money" warned Jesus. It is a total impossibility according to him. Run for all your worth from these things.

Conversely pursue, embrace, put on, run towards godliness, that is, the kingdom of God, the priorities of the King, the values of the age to come. It's a fight, it's a battle that has to be consciously engaged in every day. It is tough to go against the flow, to maintain standards, to fight the world, the flesh and the devil. But that is what it means to be a Christian warrior, a man of God.

3. The Scriptures

"All Scripture is breathed out by God and profitable for teaching, for reproof, for correction, and for training in righteousness, that the man of God may be competent, equipped for every good work." **2 Timothy 3 v 16-17**

It is by the Scriptures that the man of God is taught and by them he rebukes the world. This is a fight. We naturally prefer peace and quiet rather than contending for the faith, but this is part of the "good fight". It is not for the fainthearted. We live in days of "political correctness" when the word of God is unacceptable. The man of God stands and fights by proclaiming the truth of God's word in all kinds of situations.

The war is faced when you refuse to compromise Christian standards at work; it is faced when family deride your choice of Christian service before career; it is faced when you insist that hearing the Scriptures is more important than playing sport on Sunday. It is faced every day in every way. But it is the only life worth living!

The man of God is called to fight by prayer, by holiness of life and by the word of God; to follow the Captain of the Lord's hosts, who himself won the battle by a sacrificial bravery that took him to the cross, and who calls upon his disciples to follow him.

DISCUSS

Q1. What are the biggest challenges facing Christian men seeking to live godly lives in our culture and churches today?

Q2. What might you and a friend (or small group of men) put in place to stimulate and encourage one another to be "Christian warriors" in prayer, holiness and Scripture?

Q3. "No discipline—no discipleship" True or not? How does spiritual discipline differ from legalism, and what might it involve week by week in your life?

BIBLE STUDY

1 Timothy 4 v 6-16

In this chapter Paul is stressing to Timothy the importance of making spiritual tasks the highest priority of life.

Q1. What does it mean in practice to "train yourself for godliness" (v 7)?

Q2. Unpack the five aspects of godliness in v 12. Think about their scope and apply to your life.

Q3. According to v 15 –16, what things exactly are men to be seriously intent about in living the Christian life?

Q4. What practical changes and action will you take in response to the calling of this passage?

A full talk on this topic entitled "How to be a Christian man in the twenty-first century" is available free at www.phillipjensen.com

PART TWO:

*Living
for Christ*

3 GROWING A PERSONAL DEVOTIONAL LIFE
Men and God

John Benton

We are brought into a relationship with the living God by the gospel. And we grow in that relationship as we spend time listening to him and talking with him...

We are going to briefly explore the question of how our personal devotions can help us to become the men that God would have us be. I make three assumptions.

My first assumption is that **we can only have living contact with God through personal faith in Christ.** Our wrongdoings exclude us from God's presence, and Christ's death alone cleanses the sin of all those who believe, and makes us welcome and acceptable to God, **Hebrews 10 v 19.**

The second assumption is that **to develop a workable and profitable devotional life will involve hard work and discipline.** There are many reasons for this:

★ **SOCIAL:** Seeking God is alien to the fundamentally secular culture in which we live. The pressures of modern life tend to squeeze out the quietness and time needed to develop our relationship with God.

★ **SPIRITUAL:** Like Adam in the garden, sinful men such as us have a natural inclination to avoid our holy God.

★ **PERSONAL:** Men are, by and large, more at home on the go—
"doing things"—rather than on our knees, praying.

So in pursuing a profitable devotional life we swim against many
tides. Without a daily interaction with God, our lives will become
hollow and meaningless. But in God we find salvation, depth of
character, the renewing of our strength, and more.

The third assumption is that **the essential activities through
which we converse with God are those of Christian prayer and
Bible reading.** Our Lord Jesus was a man of prayer who knew the
Scriptures thoroughly. Through prayer we speak to God, and
through the Bible God speaks to us. These are the building blocks
of an authentic relationship with the living God. In order to
understand the unique character of our devotional life, we need
to understand a little about our distinctiveness as men.

Male Life

What makes a man? Essentially, men and women are the same.
We both rejoice in being made in God's image. But the two gen-
ders are two variations on the same theme.

The details of how the first man, Adam, was made teach us a lot.
He was created to work, so he was made strong, **Genesis 2 v 15.**
He was originally on his own, so, under God, he was made to take
initiative **Genesis 2 v 19-23.** He gave part of himself in order that
his wife, Eve, could be formed, **Genesis 2 v 21-22.** So the first man
knew how to be sacrificial. All this suggests that men are made to
work, to lead and to sacrifice themselves for the glory of God and
the good of others. It is not that women should not work, or take
initiative or give of themselves, but that these things ought to
have a certain loving prominence in the male. We must use our
strength to love as Jesus did.

With such a blueprint to follow, the immediate priority is to
have ourselves and our appetites on a short rein. Strength can easily be misused. It should not surprise us therefore that the New

Testament encourages men, particularly, to cultivate self-control, **Titus 2 v 2, 6.**

There has been much discussion recently over the perceived malaise in contemporary male lives. Is it due to the increased mobility and rootlessness in society? Does it stem from the rise of the women's movement, which encourages competition rather than harmony between the sexes? Fundamentally, it is to do with a loss of a biblical understanding of what it is to be a man. Our vocation is to be strong, self-controlled, sacrificial servant leaders.

But that throws up the real issue. Once we see what is required of men, we realise the standard is high. It is a demanding calling. We do not feel capable. We are all too aware of our sinful tendencies. So at this point many men quit. We either abandon the attempt to live God's way and just become worldly, or, ashamed of our inadequacy, we hide our real selves behind a shell of non-communication and pretence. Neither of those options will do. The answer to our weakness as men is found in a daily dependence on God—expressed through a strong devotional life with God. It is through pouring out our hearts to him in prayer, and hearing from God through his word, that we can find power to live as Christ's men.

Inner Life

Change in the Christian life must come from within. But what does the inner life, the "heart", of a human being look like? It is helpful to think about three aspects of our personality. These are the mind by which we think, the will by which we choose, and the affections by which we love.

Christians all have the Holy Spirit in their lives. Sin is a great power which, left to ourselves, we can never conquer. But there is a greater power available to us—that of God the Holy Spirit. How do we put sin to death? Paul tells us it is **"by the Spirit,"** **Romans 8 v 13.**

What does the Holy Spirit do for our inner life in respect to defeating sin? His work is not something magical or weird. Rather, he strengthens us inwardly. He gives new discernment to the mind, new determination to the will and new desire for Christ to our affections. And this relates to our devotional lives.

★ **New discernment to the mind.** The Christian apologist, Os Guinness, tells of a game he would play with his children called "spot the lie". As they watched TV adverts, if one of the youngsters could explain what was misleading in what an advert said, extra pocket money would be theirs. So they learned discernment. The Holy Spirit teaches us to spot the lie about sin. Once we perceive the poison in the doughnut, we will not eat it, no matter how enticing it looks. The Holy Spirit's first work in helping us combat sin is to give us a perceptive, discerning mind about what is right and the damage sin causes, **Philippians 1 v 9-11.** We co-operate with the Spirit in his renewing of our minds as we read and learn the Bible, the Spirit's book, **Romans 12 v 2.**

★ **New determination to the will.** Following his great sin of adultery with Bathsheba, **Psalm 51** is David's prayer of repentance. But notice what David prays there in connection with the Spirit's work in his life: "Renew a right spirit within me … Take not your Holy Spirit from me … Uphold me with a willing spirit and sustain me", v 10-12. By enabling us to "see through" temptations, and by enlarging our capacity for determination, God can give us a new steadfastness in Christian living. Here is the source of self-control for men. It is found through prayer.

★ **New desire for Christ to the affections.** The Holy Spirit enables us to feel the love of God for us and stirs our love towards the Lord Jesus Christ, **Romans 5 v 5.** Holy living needs to be motivated by love for Christ, not by some pharisaical concern to look good in front of others. How can we co-operate with the Spirit in so firing up our hearts? Surely through contemplating the love of Christ to us in a quiet time of personal devotion. The Lord's Supper can be valuable in this.

Our vocation as men is to live with a Christ-like heart, taking sacrificial initiative, to work for the glory of God and the good of others. We are naturally weak and wayward. But the energy of the Spirit, engaged through a humble devotional life, empowers us.

DEVOTIONAL LIFE

So let's look at a few "nuts and bolts" concerning building workable times of personal prayer and Bible reading into our lives.

How should I pray?

The big issues are to come to God humbly and with a forgiving attitude, trusting in the name of Jesus, **John 14 v 13-14**. Remember, we are speaking to the King of kings, who is your Father. The Lord's Prayer, **Matthew 6 v 9-13**, contains worship, and requests for provision, forgiveness, protection and the coming of God's kingdom. We should include these in the prayers we pray.

With regard to wandering thoughts, the answer can be to cultivate praying out loud. This does not mean we should bellow at God. He is not deaf! But verbalising our prayers does help concentration.

Lastly, we should give enough time to prayer. We lead busy lives. But to limit time too much will turn prayer into a formality and hinder any real engagement with God.

How should I read the Bible?

First, we must we must "put away all malice and all deceit and hypocrisy, and envy and slander," **1 Peter 2 v 1**. It is a repentant heart which benefits from the "pure spiritual milk" of the word. Second, we need to ask God's help in enlightening our understanding, **Psalm 119 v 18**. Third, we must come ready to do whatever God tells us. When Jesus was sent before Herod, who plied him with many questions, Jesus said nothing. He knew the man wasn't serious, **Luke 23 v 9**. God speaks to willing servants, not time-wasters.

If you decide to use Bible-reading notes I would suggest you use those which get you to dig out answers from the Bible text, not those which provide answers for you. With the latter, if you are not careful, you can end up being more concerned to read the notes than read the Bible.

Time?

If it's possible, the early morning is best. There are a number of reasons for this.

1. It is much easier to control this period of the day before you go out to work. Often the evening brings unexpected phone calls or legitimate demands on your time from family, friends and others which can easily wreck your schedule.
2. After an initial wake-up cup of tea, morning should be the time you are most alert. Trying to read the Bible and pray while fighting tiredness after a hard day at the office is ridiculous. Not going to bed too late helps!
3. The early hours are usually when a house is most quiet. We do not want to battle with the flat-mate's rock music or the kid's TV. If we can spend time with God more than once in a day, fine. But if your schedule means that realistically you only have one slot, go for the morning.

Place?

You need to be alone. Precisely where does not matter. The main concerns are to find somewhere quiet where you can be undisturbed. Jesus said: "Go into your room, and shut the door and pray to your Father who is in secret", **Matthew 6 v 6.** We should not pursue devotions for others to see us and think how holy we are.

Frequency?

Each day is a gift from God to us, and God should consciously be included in it. There are many encouragements in Scripture to spend time with God every day, **Psalm 145 v 2; Proverbs 8 v 34; Daniel 6 v 10; Luke 2 v 37**. Some people worry about getting into a rut by having a regular daily routine. We can face jibes about being "in slavery" to our quiet time. But spiritual "slavery" is not really about regularity of devotions. It is to do with having a legalistic outlook, which says that God will only bless you according to your efforts, rather than blessing you according to his grace. Just as there is nothing wrong and everything right with regular meals, so there is everything right about daily times of personal devotion.

The Westminster Shorter Catechism contains a wonderful sentence about the purpose of our lives. It says: "Man's chief end is to glorify God and enjoy him forever." It can be a struggle to establish and continue with a devotional life, but through personal prayer and Bible study we can both enjoy God and glorify him, not least by finding the resources to become the men he wants us to be.

Real lives

Rob has been an officer in the Army for six years and his job has led him into active service in Northern Ireland and Kosovo. He knew from the start that if he was to survive as a Christian in the Army, devotional time would be crucial. "Joining the Army is a bit like your first day at college or starting a new job—you need to nail your colours to the mast from day one and live by your convictions. If you don't, you are compromised immediately and your faith quickly starts to slip away."

Although routine is part of life in the Army, Rob has to work hard to protect his quiet times, and makes the most of every opportunity to pray with and encourage other Christians he comes across. "I try to get all the help I can to keep my faith strong—emails and text messages from Christian mates, reading Christian books and listening to tapes, carrying memory verses on cards—I even write a verse in my diary for each day! I also find that telling others about what I believe confirms it for me and reminds me exactly why I'm following Christ."

There have been times when Rob has struggled to remain strong. "In the Army your comfort zones are taken away and you often feel out of your depth. At those times you either sharpen your faith, or your faith dies. God has taught me that if I cry out to him, then I can depend on him absolutely to sustain me."

Real lives

What happens if you really can't fit in a morning devotional time?

Phil is a contracts manager for a landscaping company. He is married with two lively children. His job involves managing between 20 and 30 men, and that means being at the office by 7.15am and rarely being home before 6.30pm. Most afternoons he is out on the road visiting clients and staff at various locations many miles from home.

Phil's day begins by getting up and making tea at 6am. Over breakfast he and his wife like to briefly read the Bible and pray together. They pray for two topics a day (work and neighbours on Monday, etc) and for the people of their church. Then it's off to work.

So where does Phil fit in his personal devotions? His solution is to use his lunch break. Out on the road, he takes a sandwich and a flask from home. On his way to his afternoon visits he pulls up somewhere quiet. "The car becomes my sanctuary," says Phil. Often he can spend 30 minutes with the Lord, surrounded by the relative peace of a forest. He comments: "If I don't do this, I find I'm walking by sight and not by faith."

DISCUSS

Q1. What obstacles do you face (social, spiritual, personal) in having a regular "quiet time"?

Q2. How can you encourage yourself, and others, to be more disciplined about spending time with the Lord?

Q3. "Men are made to work, to lead and to sacrifice themselves for the glory of God and the good of others." Which do you struggle with most?

BIBLE STUDY

Psalm 1

Q1. Look at v 1. What are the common sources of "the counsel of the wicked" these days?

Q2. Eastern meditation involves emptying the mind, but Christian meditation (v 2) means focusing the mind on God's word and thinking it through. What are the benefits according to v 3? Why does God's word produce such good results in us?

Q3. From v 4-6 how would you describe the two possible destinations for life's journey? Why is taking notice of the Bible so vital?

4 "CURSE OR OPPORTUNITY?"

Men and singleness

Vaughan Roberts

There is much Christian literature that focuses on marriage and the family, but very little that focuses on singleness. And yet most of us will be single for most of our lives...

About 35% of adult church members in Britain are single, so clearly the subject of singleness is of considerable personal interest to many men in our churches. Each will have a slightly different experience of singleness. There are age differences. Being single at 20 is very different from being single at 30, 40 or 70. There are circumstantial differences: some have never married, others are divorcees or widowers. And there are experiential differences: some have chosen to be single and are basically content; others long to be married and feel frustrated. What does the Bible say to all these people?

1. Singleness is a gift from God

So much in our society is structured around couples. It is often just assumed that adults will have a partner, and that there is something rather odd about them if they do not for any period of time. Oscar Wilde summed up the view of many: "Celibacy is the only known sexual perversion". There is nothing new in this negative view of celibacy. Rabbi Eleazar said in the first century: "Any man who has no wife is no proper man". The Jewish writings known as the Talmud went even further: "The man who is not married at twenty is living in sin". Given that background, it is astonishing how positive the New Testament is about singleness. Paul speaks of it as a "gift" (1 **Corinthians** 7 v 7) and Jesus says that it is good for "those to whom it is given" (**Matthew 19 v 11**).

A friend of mine once belonged to a church young adults' group which had the name: "Pairs and Spares". Single people can be made to feel like spare parts in their families, social groups and churches. One man I know was so fed up with being asked: "Are you still single?" that he began to respond with: "Are you still married?" We must resist the implication that singleness is second best: the Bible does not think so. Marriage is good, but so is singleness: it has been "given" to some.

But what if I do not think that I have the "gift" of singleness? I do not find it easy being on my own and I long to marry; surely that means that I am experiencing second best? The answer is a resounding "No". When Paul speaks of singleness as a gift, he is not speaking about a particular ability that some people have to be contentedly single. He is, rather, speaking of the state of being single. For as long as you have it, that is a gift from God, just as marriage will be God's gift if you ever receive it. We should receive our situation in life, whether it is singleness or marriage, as a gift of God's grace to us.

2. Singleness is beneficial

Paul mentions two advantages of singleness in **1 Corinthians 7**:

★ Single people are spared the "troubles" of marriage. There are many great blessings in marriage, but there are difficulties too. Understandably, Christian couples do not often talk openly about the hard things they face. That can give those who are single a rose-tinted view of marriage. But there is a down-side even when a couple's relationship is good. Life is more complicated for those who are married. There is more than one person to consider in decisions about use of time, accommodation, holidays, and even the daily menu. And there is more than one person to worry about. Children bring great pleasure, and plenty of anxiety as well. Marriage brings "many troubles in this life" and, says Paul, "I would spare you this" (v 28). He mentions these troubles here chiefly because of the bearing they have on the next point.

★ Single people are able to devote themselves to God's work: "The unmarried man is anxious about worldly things, how to please the Lord. But the married man is anxious about worldly things, how to please his wife, and his interests are divided" (v 32-34). A very important part of the Christian responsibility of men who are married is to care for their wife and children. That should take time: time that can not therefore be spent in witnessing to people, helping out on a camp, doing the church finances or leading a Bible study. Single people have more time to give to such things. It is no coincidence that many activities in church life depend to a large extent on those who are not married. A few consciously choose to stay single to devote themselves to Christian work. Most single people have not chosen singleness in that way and yet they have just the same advantages as those who have. Instead of focusing on the difficulties of being single, as some do, we should all make the most of the advantages of God's gift of singleness while we have it.

3. Singleness is hard

When God saw Adam on his own in the Garden of Eden he said: "It is not good that the man should be alone. I will make him a helper fit for him" (Gen 2 v 18). So Eve was created to meet Adam's need for companionship and the two came together in the lifelong, sexual relationship of marriage. Although the New Testament is positive about singleness, there is no doubt that marriage is regarded as the norm. It is God's loving gift to humanity and is the chief context in which our desire for intimacy is met. Single people are therefore likely to struggle with loneliness and sexual temptation. Those struggles are certainly not exclusive to the unmarried but they are very much a part of the single condition. Some will seek to lessen them by getting married. Others will either choose not to marry or will feel unable to because of their circumstances, personality or sexual orientation. They are likely to face a lifelong battle with loneliness and sexual temptation.

Those two battles are closely related. The more lonely we are, the more likely we are to struggle with sexual fantasy and fall into sin. We need to be proactive in helping ourselves in these areas. We are not designed to be on our own and if we are not to be married, whether in the short or long term, we should seek to satisfy our need for intimacy in other relationships. That will mean taking the initiative in keeping in close contact with friends and family. And we must be self-disciplined to "flee from sexual immorality" (I Corinthians 6 v 18). It often helps to have one or two close friends to whom we are accountable in this area.

4. Singleness is temporary

Many of those who are presently single will subsequently marry. Others will remain single throughout their lives. But no Christian is single for ever. Human marriage is a reflection of the marriage God wants to enjoy with his people for ever. The Bible speaks of Jesus as the bridegroom who will one day return to take his bride, the church, to be with him in the perfect new creation. On that day all pain will disappear, including the pain of a difficult marriage or singleness. God will wipe away every tear from our eyes, and a great shout will be heard: "Let us rejoice and exult and give him the glory, for the marriage of the Lamb has come, and his Bride has made herself ready" (Rev 7 v 17; 19 v 7). Once, after I had spoken on this subject, an elderly single lady said to me: "I can't wait for my wedding day!" We should all share the same hope. And we can already experience something of that intimate marriage with Christ here on earth by the work of the Spirit in our lives. Human relationships *do* matter, but none is nearly as important as our eternal relationship with Christ.

A final word to those who are single:
- ★ **Thank God for the gift of singleness.** Whatever your experience of singleness, recognise it as a gift from God and make the most of it for as long as you have it.
- ★ **Do all you can to be godly.** It is very easy for those who are single to lapse into a selfish, self-centred lifestyle and into sexual sin, whether in thought or deed. Be self-disciplined and accountable to others.
- ★ **Keep your eyes fixed on heaven.** It is our eternal relationship with Christ that ultimately matters.

A final word to those who are married:
- ★ **Do not think of singleness as second best.** Evangelist John Chapman tells of friends taking him for long walks, telling him he should be married. He comments: "It would have been a great help if they had read the Bible, wouldn't it?"
- ★ **Remember that your family is the whole church.** There should be no lonely people in our church. We need to be opening up our homes to one another and relating to one another, not just in the nuclear family, but in the church family.
- ★ **Keep your eyes fixed on heaven.** Human marriage matters, but it will not last for ever **(Mark 12 v 25)**. Our relationship with Christ must come first.

Real lives

Dave is a manager in a manufacturing company based in a large city.

He is 33, and although he would prefer to be married he just hasn't found the right person. Some might say he is a perfectionist, but the busyness of his life has meant that he hasn't allowed much time for chasing a partner.

Dave sees singleness as a challenge to remain content in all circumstances. "People often view singleness as a disease, thinking that if you're not married, you're only half a person. But that's ridiculous! If we believe in the inspiration of Scripture, then marriage on this earth is just a little experience of the awesome marriage that happens with Christ when we get to heaven."

But he admits that he has to take concrete steps to remain contented and avoid temptation. "I find it helpful to keep up close friendships with married friends so that I don't over-romanticize marriage and can see the sacrifices and common struggles that they have to make. I also find it easier not to have a TV, and if I find I have a free Saturday night, I often take the initiative early in the week to ring up friends and make plans. Singleness is fine six days a week, but it's on that seventh random day, when you might really wish you were in a relationship, that you need to be proactive in managing loneliness and avoiding temptation to be immoral."

Of course, being single means that Dave has more free time, which he values greatly. "I try to rejoice in the good things that God has given me and ultimately I know that it is Christ who can meet all my needs—not the good job or the great relationship. The challenge is to realise that life is short, and there is no point sitting around worrying about the things you don't have. A wise Christian minister once advised me: "Getting married means you swap one set of problems for another". While this seems to be true for most, I still think that marriage is a better way of life. In God's sovereignty I hope to have the chance to marry. However, contentment is a spiritual discipline and those that are discontent before marriage seem also to be discontent when married. The challenge is to trust God—please pray that I continue to seek his kingdom first."

DISCUSS

Q1. Does your church or social group esteem singleness and the single? Why do they take this view? How could you develop and display a more positive view of singleness?

Q2. In what areas of single life am I struggling to be holy?

Q3. How can married men be more inclusive of single people (of all ages) without being condescending?

Q4. How can single and unmarried people deal with sexual temptation? How can they lessen the risks? How can they increase their self-control?

BIBLE STUDY

1 Corinthians 7

Q1. What basic principles does Paul teach from verses 17-24 about marriage and singleness?

Q2. From v 32-35, what are the advantages of being single?

Q3. How can I best use my current status to "please the Lord"?

Matthew 19 v 8-12

Q4. Does Jesus suggest you need more of a special gift to be married or to be single?

Q5. What is God's solution for someone who is unhappily single or unhappily married?

Q6. If you want to get married, but can't find a partner, are you just being too fussy? If not, why do you think it is that you are still single?

5 THE COURAGEOUS HUSBAND

Men and marriage

David Jackman

The Bible encourages men to view their role in marriage as being a sacrificial leader. How does this work out in practice...?

I have been married to Heather for over 30 years, but when she saw the title of the chapter I had been asked to write for this book, her first response was: "Well, what does that say about me!?" I was happy to assure her that this was no comment about our marriage—but that all Christian men need spiritual courage to order our marriages in accordance with God's principles laid down in the teaching of the Bible.

The basic issue

In its opening chapters, the Bible addresses the most personal and intimate human relationship we shall ever be in, not only because it is so central to our experience of life, but also because marriage is God's idea. It is his good gift to humankind, not our invention. That is why we can go back with confidence to the Maker's instructions. Indeed, we must do that, if ever the gift is going to function as God intended.

Because such an idea is profoundly counter-cultural, Christian men need courage to swim against the tide. Magazines and newspapers, films and TV programmes all loudly proclaim that human nature is infinitely plastic. You can bend it and shape it any which way you like. There are no absolute standards of behaviour, so there are no principles to govern marriage or any other areas of human activity. If it feels OK, then it is OK—at least for you, provided no one else gets hurt in the process, or at least not too badly. However, Christians believe that as created beings we can only function properly when we operate in the way the Creator has "wired us up". And that's why **Genesis 1 v 26-28** is so important.

At the very beginning of human life, we learn that the totality of God's image in humanity requires both male and female to be complete. The uniqueness of human beings is that we are made to think, to choose, to love and to worship God. In all of these areas there is an equality before God, irrespective of gender, and an equality of role in God's world (**v 28**). Both male and female are to be fruitful, to increase and to rule over God's world, but within that divinely-given unity there is the difference of gender and sexuality, which is also God's gift.

Not surprisingly, in **Genesis 2 v 18** the fact of marriage is given the same importance as the fact of creation. "It is not good that the man should be alone," God says. "I will make him a helper fit for him." Everything in creation has been judged "good" in chapter 1, but this is "not good". So, as evidence of his care for man, God acts on his own unique understanding and wisdom to provide an exact match, a partner or helper made to measure. From this, several inferences need to be drawn.

Husband and wife are **complementary** to each other in their different roles within marriage. To be the "helper" is not a mark of inferiority, since God himself is frequently described as the "helper" of Israel. "For this reason (the creation of woman) a man will leave his father and mother and be united to his wife, and they will become one flesh" **(Genesis 2 v 24)**. This is the priority above all other human relationships; expressed in the depth of union ("one flesh"), in its exclusivity ("his wife") and its permanence ("be united"). This last verb is the strongest adhesive word in the whole of the Old Testament.

In **Genesis 3**, the event of the Fall turns, at least in part, on a reversal of roles. Eve is beguiled and deceived, by the serpent's clever words, to put her own desires and values above God's word. Adam needs no such deception. He is happy to go along with the rebellion quite openly and defiantly (v 6). But the consequences of the Fall are devastating, not least with regard to marriage. As always in the Bible, the outworking is peculiarly related to the nature of the offence. Because the woman usurped her role, from helper to initiator/ leader, the man will tend to re-assert his leadership in dominating and tyrannous ways.

Because the man "obeyed" his wife and ate the forbidden fruit, he will only eat his daily bread as the result of painful toil. Every act of disobedience perpetuates the same effects, so the foundational marriage relationship was skewed by and in the Fall itself, and, ever since, marriages have been in trouble.

"If love is blind," it is said, "then marriage is a great eye-opener". In his book *The Five Love Languages* (Northfield Publications, Chicago 1992) Gary Chapman writes: "Once the experience of falling in love has run its natural course (remember, the average in-love experience lasts two years), we will return to the world of reality and begin to assert ourselves. He will express his desires, but his desires will be different from hers." We should not be surprised if marriage exposes our selfishness more ruthlessly and tests our character more demandingly than any other relationship. That is why the best marriages take a lot of work, intentional effort and commitment, on both sides. But it is also true that marriage is one of the clearest and most persuasive areas of life in which we can see the enormous difference Christ and the gospel make to the norms of human behaviour.

The controlling pattern

Ephesians 5 v 21 is the greatest New Testament passage about marriage. It begins with a mutual submission which reflects the foundational, personal submission of both husband and wife to Christ. It expresses their readiness to live by the divinely-given pattern which follows. Indeed, this was one of the main ways in which the gospel demonstrated its life-transforming power in pagan Ephesus, a city dominated by the feminist cult of Diana, the mother goddess. In the similar cultural climate of today, the Bible's teaching is often rejected out of hand, just as it was then. But what is Paul actually teaching?

In **verse 23**, he speaks of the "headship" of the husband. The ultimate responsibility, before God, for our marriages and families rests on the shoulders of the husbands. In this context, wives are to submit (**v 22**) as they do to Christ. It is the lordship of Christ which is the parallel developed in this section (**v 24**), pointing to his ultimate responsibility for his people. A Christian husband's model as to how he should relate to his wife is how Christ relates to him. His lordship is entirely experienced as love, continually working for the greatest benefit of each of us as his disciples. This love is the context and manner in which "headship" is to be exercised (**v 25**). So this cannot be mere words, or moments of passion, but a consistent and determined policy to do everything for the loved one's greatest good. Ultimately, Christ loved the church so much that he sacrificed his very life for her.

This pattern is profoundly counter-cultural. All around us voices encourage us to claim our rights, to ask: "What am I getting out of this? Am I being appreciated or fulfilled?" But marriage is not so much a matter of rights as responsibilities for one another. Doesn't the marriage service promise: "All that I have, I give to you, and all that I am, I share with you"? A Christian husband is committed to developing his wife's unique potential to the maximum, especially in spiritual matters (**v 26-27**). He should take the initiative in spiritual leadership, praying together and reading

Scripture, setting the example to his family of real discipleship, nourishing and cherishing his wife, as Christ does him (**v 28-29**). When a husband loves his wife so wholeheartedly and is so good a husband to her, she won't find submission a problem and neither will he!

Paul's emphasis is on the husband's role because of his responsibility to lead. So many frustrated wives end up "wearing the trousers" because their husbands won't. Of course, every marriage has to work out its own pattern of roles and duties, and we do not have to submit to sub-cultural stereotypes, but the principle is totally revolutionary. **You never gain by getting—only by giving.** The headship-in-love principle produces 100% commitment on both sides, because the greatest killer of marriage is self-love. So, when problems occur, we first need to examine our own selfishness, before criticising or condemning our partner.

The key areas

Communication must come first. Marriage will raise differences of view and opinions in many areas of life, but the danger is not in the issues themselves so much as an unwillingness to talk them through. All sorts of differences can become areas of conflict, because misunderstanding and resentment build through non-communication. Men need to be aware that women usually feel the relationship is going well if we are talking, whereas men tend to think that if we need to talk it must be going badly! Women usually deal with their problems by sharing them, whereas men often retreat into their "cave" to sort them out alone. A good marriage will require good talking time, which is usually not after 11pm!

But communication has to be fostered and encouraged. It is all too often assassinated by one of three common weapons—anger, tears and silence. Explosive anger is usually self-protective. It says: "You can't get that close to me and say those things". Tears can be equally manipulative. How many men say: "I can't cope with her when she goes to pieces, so it's not worth the hassle"? But silence, although it can seem pious, is actually lethal. We have to speak the truth, in love (**Ephesians 4 v 15**)—please note that it is both! The more you want to tell your wife the truth, the more love you need in conveying it.

Pray about the right, relaxed opportunities to speak. Seek God's wisdom about how you say what you say. Say what's on your mind clearly and tenderly, but allow time for reaction. Never be slow to apologise, to ask for forgiveness or to express your love—love that is patient, kind, generous, humble, courteous, considerate, unselfish, guileless and sincere.

Conflict-resolution is also an area in which the husband should take the lead. We need to establish the facts in any issue, but without disregarding the feelings that attach to them. You may think they are irrational, but they are real. We need to listen, observe and understand. We don't need to have an immediate solution to every problem. Try, rather, to sort out the real points at issue. Are there clear biblical principles of right and wrong, or just personal preferences, expressive of temperament and upbringing? Are they central or marginal, temporary or long-lasting? Difficulties can be resolved if there is a willingness to break habitual patterns and look for new ways to help each other. Never be ashamed to ask for help, but try not to be problem-dominated. Work on the why and how, rather than rehearsing accusations and recriminations.

Spiritual well-being remains the greatest need. My wife and my children are my primary and life-long commitments before God, and therefore should have priority over both my work and church relationships, in terms of commitment and investment. For this to happen, God must come first, because I will love my wife best by loving God first, and she will love me best in exactly the same way. But we husbands do need to keep asking the key check-up questions:

★ Am I giving my marriage and home life quality time, or just the left-overs of the day?

★ Is my wife still the most important person in my life? Does she know it?

★ Am I supporting her sufficiently with the children and their spiritual development?

★ What initiatives am I taking to help us both grow in our knowledge and love of God?

It is the easiest thing in the world to duck out, plead overwork, hope for the best—but actually to dodge our responsibilities and to weaken our marriages. We need courage to swim against the cynicism of our culture, to affirm marriage as God's good gift, and with his help to build, with strength and fulfilment, godly marriages, as examples of his wonderful patience and limitless grace.

"Be watchful, stand firm in the faith, act like men, be strong. Let all that you do be done in love." **(1 Corinthians 16 v 13-14)**

DISCUSS

Q1. Many men are the "strong, silent type".
What efforts are you making to communicate more with your wife?

Q2. Do you set aside time to pray with your wife?
What is preventing you from this?

Q3. How can you help your wife grow as a Christian? Are there any areas that you need to review and change?

6 "GOOD SEX?"

Men and sex

Tim Chester

Sex within marriage? Yes. Sex is a wonderful and powerful act that binds couples together. But outside the covenant commitments of marriage its power becomes the power to harm. Paul calls it a sin against our own bodies (**1 Corinthians 6 v 18**).

The Bible portrays sex as a great gift from God. Its prohibition on sex outside of marriage is not to protect us from sex, but to protect sex from us. That prohibition is like the banks that hold in the spectacular torrent of water that is Niagara Falls. Take the prohibition away and you're left with something more like the Mississippi Delta—wide, shallow and muddy.

But there's more to be said about good sex. Because not all sex within marriage is good sex. So is good sex defined by the level of gymnastics or the intensity of orgasm? Not quite. Sex is not a performance.

Sex and self-giving

To work out what constitutes good sex we need to know what sex is for. Only then can we judge whether it's achieving its purpose. John Piper says "sexuality is designed by God as a way to know God in Christ more fully" and "knowing God in Christ more fully is designed as a way of guarding and guiding our sexuality". He bases this on the Bible's repeated link between God's relationship to his people and a sexual relationship. It's not only when sexuality works as it should within marriage that it helps us know God in Christ (**Ephesians 5 v 22-33**). The pain of adultery points to the nature of sin against God (**Ezekiel 16**) while the emptiness and futility felt in singleness or multiple sexual encounters points to the true fulness that Christ alone gives us (**John 4 v 4-26**).

So good sex is sex within marriage that enables us to know God in Christ more fully, or sex within marriage that reflects the relationship of God in Christ to his people. Immediately this enables us to define some characteristics of good sex: good sex is intimate, affectionate, gentle, sacrificial, personal and pleasurable. Sex teaches us the pleasure of self-giving: the pleasure of giving pleasure, the love of loving, the honour of honouring, the blessing of being a blessing.

The model of Christ's relationship to his church means that central to sex is self-giving. The very act of sex is a deep disclosure of ourselves. We're offering our wife, as it were, not only a view of our bodies, but a view of our souls. Sex is an act of union.

It is becoming one flesh.

And it can only achieve this purpose if there is self-giving.

Sex and idolatry

That which most threatens our relationship with God—our idolatry—is that which most threatens good sex. Idolatry is often likened to adultery in the Bible. Idolatry is to give our allegiance and love to another just as in adultery we give our allegiance and love to another.

Consider how idolatrous desires can corrupt sex within marriage.

When you don't get enough sex

It's all too common to find a tension between husband and wife over how often they have sex, usually with the husband wanting sex more often than his wife. Men typically blame their wives. But more often than not the real problem is that *sex has become an idol*. Sex itself, or sexual pleasure, matters more to us than honouring God by sacrificially loving our partner. Our allegiance to sex is greater than our allegiance to God. We love sex more than we love our wives.

We need to put our wife's desires above our own desires. It might mean saying: "Thank you for offering to have sex tonight, but we're both a bit tired. How about we have an early night tomorrow and just have a cuddle and chat tonight?" Think what that communicates to your wife?

If sex is what matters most, then you will begin making love by removing your clothes. But if serving you partner is what matters most, then you'll "make love" throughout the day through little acts of service, words of kindness, gestures of affection. Men typically see intimacy in physical terms, but often what matters more to wives is verbal communication. Al Mohler suggests a husband must "earn access to the marriage bed".

When I say that a husband must regularly "earn" privileged access to the marital bed, I mean that a husband owes his wife the confidence, affection, and emotional support that would lead her to freely give herself to him in the act of sex. God's gift of sexuality is inherently designed to pull us out of ourselves and towards our spouse. For men, this means that marriage calls us out of our self-focused concern for genital pleasure and towards the totality of the sex act within the marital relationship.

Making love without making love

Any sex in which we objectify our wife is bad sex. Again, sex itself has become more important than honouring God by serving our partner. We objectify our partner when we consider them a means by which we can gain sexual pleasure rather than a person with whom we have a relationship. This can occur if we put our pleasure above theirs. Or it can occur if, through fantasy, we transpose ourselves into another situation or imagine having sex with

Jack and Emma have been married for fifteen years.

"Sex was a massive source of tension in our marriage for years," says Jack. "Basically I wanted more sex than Emma. She felt under pressure which only made matters worse. I got frustrated. She felt even more pressure. It was a vicious cycle." What made the difference?

"I remember thinking one day after we'd had a row that I loved sex more than Emma."

Sex had become an idol. Sex mattered more to Jack than honouring God by serving Emma. "Obviously I still have my moments," he says. "But there's been a massive change. I'm starting to get sex in perspective. I've realised it was more about me feeling manly than anything else. Seems a bit pathetic when you put it like that. And Emma's relaxed a whole more and we're having better sex."

another partner. Asking our wife to wear lingerie or special clothing (dressing up as a nurse, for example) is another form of objectification if it's intended to transform our wife temporarily into someone else. When this occurs, we are committing adultery even as we have sex with our own partner.

When they don't seem up for it

Another common complaint of husbands is that wives are not "up for it". Your wife is willing to have sex with you. She's happy to serve you and give you pleasure through sex. But tonight she's not that interested in her own sexual pleasure. But this is not enough for you. You wants a sexually rapacious wife!

"I only want to give her pleasure," more than one husband has said to me. "What's wrong with that?" But maybe the truth is that you want to be worshipped by your wife. You want her to acknowledge your sexual prowess and power, to be helpless before you as she's overwhelmed by her desire for you. This is idolatry. You want to be worshipped as a sex god.

Or one of you may resent "planning" sex or always having sex in the same context. You long for moments when you're both overcome by desire. There's nothing wrong with spontaneity or variation, but resentment when they're lacking is a sign that something is amiss. It may reflect a desire for moments when your wife falls under your power and worships you.

An obsession with "serving" or "pleasuring" your wife can in fact be self-serving. You want to be worshipped. You want to feel potent. And when you are not worshipped in this way, then you complain that your wife is not "up for it".

This means that serving your partner may involve allowing them the pleasure of serving you even when they don't feel up for sex. This is truly humbling. We don't like to think that our partners are only having sex with us because they want to serve us (out of pity, we might caricature it). But one of the joys of a godly marriage is that we *find* pleasure in *giving* pleasure.

This reciprocal giving of pleasure and accepting of pleasure—of finding pleasure through accepting pleasure—reflects our relationship with God. In love the pleasure of God and our pleasure cohere. God delights in our delight in him. We delight in God's delight in us.

Good sex is good sex

Good sex (God-honouring sex) should lead to good sex (pleasurable sex). Sex will always be best when both partners are self-giving, pursuing the pleasure of their partner above their own pleasure. But the aim of God-honouring sex is not to achieve a better orgasm. It's not a technique for personal fulfilment or even marital fulfilment. The aim of good sex is that God is honoured. Godliness is its own reward. Yet, as is so often the case in the Christian life, we find that in losing our lives and denying ourselves, we in fact gain our lives.

There are two basic problems in every marriage: one is the husband and the other is the wife. We are all selfish, sinful human beings who want the world to revolve around us—and marriage throws us together in close proximity. Our idolatrous desires both clash and reinforce one another. Because sex-problems arise from the idolatrous desires of our hearts, their solution is faith and repentance. In faith we reaffirm that God is bigger and better than our idolatrous desires—and in repentance we put God and his glory back at the centre of lives.

But what about other aspects of sex that are not God honouring? There are three that often trouble men, and need to be discussed.

1. Masturbation

This is often thought of as something that plagues young single men, but there are many married men who continue to masturbate in later life. The Bible doesn't directly talk about masturbation. But when you think about masturbating, consider the following.

First, it's a sin to have sex with someone other than your spouse, even if that sex takes place only in your mind (**Matthew 5 v 27-30**). The fact is that masturbation is all but impossible without sexual fantasies, and you need to be confident that whatever fantasies are in your mind as you masturbate are honouring to God.

Secondly, masturbation is often justified as something that gives a physical "release" to men who are frustrated through lack of sex, and that it is harmless and "healthy." The problem is that masturbation *doesn't* relieve sexual tension, except on the most short-term basis. It actually fuels it. It reinforces sexual thoughts and so usually makes temptation come back sooner and stronger. This is why many people think they can't stop masturbating. Masturbation *increases the hold of lust over your life*. It's not solving anything. In fact, it's making the problem worse.

Thirdly, masturbation doesn't involve the self-giving that is integral to sexual intercourse. There are exceptions to this (mutual masturbation within marriage during illness or as part of fertility treatment), but for the most part it's an act of *self-love* not an act of loving someone else.

At best, then, masturbation is fraught with danger. To use biblical language: "'All things are lawful for me,' but not all things are helpful. 'All things are lawful for me,' but I will not be enslaved by anything." (**1 Corinthians 6 v 12**)

So ask yourself the following questions:

- *Does my masturbation involve inappropriate sexual fantasies?*
- *Am I in control of my masturbation or am I being mastered by it?*
- *Is my masturbation beneficial? Does it strengthen my marriage? Does it enhance my relationship with God?*

You may have been masturbating for years. It may have become the normal way you relieve tension, boredom or stress. Life without it seems inconceivable. But I've found many men can stop habitual masturbation more readily than they imagine. Every act of resistance strengthens their resolve for next time. Holiness becomes reinforcing.

2. Pornography

A number of surveys suggest about one in two Christian men are struggling with porn. This is a massive issue, yet one about which we rarely talk.

There are a number of things we can do to avoid temptation—like putting accountability software on our computers or not watching late-night television alone. You won't beat porn without putting measures like these in place. But they're not enough to deal with the real problem. We are changed by faith, not law.

What does that mean with porn? Faith sees through the false promises that porn makes to us. And faith sees that God offers us far more than porn can ever deliver.

Porn promises refuge

For many people porn is a place of refuge when we feel over-whelmed or defeated. We enter a fantasy world in which we're successful, adored, in control. The act of looking at porn rein-forces this as I search for women who are all available to me. But it's a fantasy. Instead of turning to porn when we feel over-whelmed, we should turn to God. David describes God as his rock, fortress, deliverer, refuge, stronghold (**Psalm 18 v 1-2**). *Porn prom-ises refuge. We counter this with faith in God's greatness.*

Porn promises respect

I project myself onto the porn star and vicariously experience his potency. I'm impressive, respected, worshipped, adored. But again it's a fantasy. We want the approval of other people. The Bible calls this "the fear of man" and the answer is the fear of the LORD. He is the One whose opinion should matter to us. *Porn promises respect. We counter this with faith in God's glory.*

Porn promises reward

Some people turn to porn simply because it's pleasurable. Porn is a reward we've earned or a quick fix. But then what? It's legacy is emptiness, guilt, shame. That's why porn is addictive: it leaves you wanting more. More porn. More extremes.

Jesus promises the woman at a well in Samaria living water (**John 4 v 4-26**). He knows she's had five husbands plus one. This woman has been looking for meaning, satisfaction and fulfilment in sex. But they're like water that leaves her thirsty again. Jesus offers true and lasting joy, "a spring of water welling up to eternal life" (v 14). *Porn promises reward. We counter this with faith in God's goodness.*

Porn promises revenge

Porn can be an expression of anger, resentment, ingratitude. It may be an act against your wife, perhaps when sex is not forth-coming, or against God when life hasn't turned out the way we want. Why should I be pure when God doesn't deliver? But thankfully God doesn't treat us on a contractual basis. He doesn't give us what we deserve (condemnation). He gives us what Christ deserves (righteousness). *Porn promise revenge. We counter this with faith in God's grace.*

At the heart of porn is self-worship. It offers a world in which people worship me. Porn is a sin of the imagination. We need to counter it by letting the truth capture our imaginations. We need to feel the truth, glory in the truth, delight in the truth. Remind yourself of Christ's goodness, glory, grace and greatness until your heart is warmed again by those truths and Christ is supreme in your heart. We don't just say to ourselves: "I should not use porn". The good news is that we can say to ourselves: "I need not use porn because God is bigger and better than porn".

And tell someone about it. Porn thrives on secrecy. Bring it into the light. Too afraid? Then your reputation matters more to you than your holiness. Be a man. Find someone who will hold you accountable and speak the truth of the gospel to your heart.

3. Homosexuality
Some men are plagued by homosexual temptations. Many of us will have experienced same-sex attractions when we were adolescents, but it is not unusual for these feelings to continue into adulthood.

The good news is that nothing is beyond God's forgiveness because of the cross of Christ. But we need to commit ourselves to recognizing sin as sin, and turning from it with the help of God and each other. In all these struggles, it can be truly liberating to know that you are not struggling alone. Honest, gracious, supportive friendship with a Christian brother can be an enormous help.

There are a number of helpful Christian organisations which specialise in supporting Christians struggling with these issues.

BIBLE STUDY

1 Corinthians 6 v 9-20

Q1. What attitudes to sex do you come across in the world around you? Are any of these attitudes similar to the slogans of Corinth (v 12-13)?

Q2. How does Paul counter these attitudes?

Q3. We can make sex a way to find "salvation" in the sense of fulfilment or a substitute for satisfaction in God. Can you see this in your life or the life of others around you?

Q4. What is Paul's response in 1 Corinthians 6?

1 Corinthians 7 v 1-5

Q5. How can Christians overreact to the permissive culture around them?

Q6. What is Paul's response to people advocating celibacy?

Q7. Who owns your body if you are married (see 6 v 13 and 7 v 4). What does this mean in practice?

DISCUSS

Q1. Are porn and sexual temptation talked about in your church? What could you do to create a culture of accountability and support?

Q2. What do sexual fantasies or porn offer you? How does God offer more?

Q3. What kinds of temptation are you particularly vulnerable to? Discuss ways that you can help yourself and each other to resist.

Q3. What strategies for avoiding sexual temptation are you putting in place?

Q3. How would your church help someone who struggles with homosexual temptations?

If you are married, use reading this book as a reason to ask your wife what she thinks about your relationships and your sex life.

7 "ROCK AND ROLE?"

Men and fatherhood

Trevor Archer

Fathers are often portrayed as weak, irresponsible, selfish and useless. But for the Christian man, God himself is to be our model for responsible fatherhood.

1. The biblical foundation – God the Father

In the Bible God reveals himself as "Father". At the heart of this fatherhood lie three key activities namely: **Giving life**, **Owning responsibility** and **Living sacrificially**.

Giving life: God is the "Father" of the world, of Israel, of Jesus and of the church; the One by whom every family on earth is "named" (**Ephesians 3**). Just as a human father imparts something of himself to his offspring, so God does to his creation and his creatures. The created world displays something of the power and glory of God the Creator. Humanity, made in the "image of God", uniquely bears something of the divine nature. Consequently, an important distinctive of the human father is that of implanting the seed and initiating life. Fathers have the awesome privilege of initiating life.

Owning responsibility: The Father, the source of life, takes responsibility for the life he has created. He sustains, provides, protects and cares for his creation and his creatures, daily involved in the wellbeing and ordering of his world.

Consequently, human fathers have the responsibility of providing and caring for their children. Mayor Rudi Giuliani, famed for his leadership in the aftermath of September 11, has a famous sign on his desk: "I'm Responsible!"—a principle drilled into him by his father. It is a concept derived from God's fatherhood, which he has created human fathers to reflect.

This, in turn, leads to **Living sacrificially**: In the pursuit of the eternal wellbeing of his family, God gave his very best. He made the supreme sacrifice. "God so loved the world, that he gave his only Son" (**John 3 v 16**). This sacrificial element is integral to a biblical view of fatherhood. Before the Fall, Adam allows something to be taken from him in order to create Eve, to create family. Consequently, human fathers have the awesome opportunity of making sacrifices for the good of their children; and strength for service and brave deeds.

2. The battles fathers face

There are two major deterrents to such a model of true fatherhood:

The fallen nature within us. At the heart of Adam's sin in the Garden was an abdication of his God-given responsibility to lead. It remains a core problem for men. The temptation to stand back, to cop out, to pass up on responsibility—not least when it comes to taking the lead in the spiritual wellbeing of our wives and children—is ever present.

The selfish culture around us. We face the challenge of raising children in a culture where the break up of family, the absence or disengagement of fathers—and the consequential wounding of spirits—the feminist attack on masculinity, and the post-modern outlook are accepted as the "norm".

Think how the male/female order is often portrayed in TV adverts. The dumb, inadequate, lazy and incompetent father. In contrast there's the able, confident woman who is, (in the case of the car ads), well and truly in the driving seat. The message is clear. Men are essentially inept and unreliable. The result is a profound uncertainty among men as to what it means to be male today.

This sinful tendency to abdicate responsibility, coupled to the undermining effects of a godless culture, are a lethal cocktail. They present a massive challenge to Christian men and fathers. Amazing therefore that, in the face of such peril, the New Testament's main body of practical advice on fatherhood is contained in just eighteen words!

"Fathers, do not exasperate your children, instead bring them up in the training and instruction of the Lord." **Ephesians 6 v 4**

3. *The biblical aim of fatherhood*

Christian parenting is not about getting your child to adhere to some Christianised rules and regulations—it is about nurturing in them a relationship with God. It is essentially a battle for the heart. It is not merely about producing good behaviour or good citizens but growing godly men and women who have a heart for God and an appetite for his kingdom purposes. Anything else is second best and is to miss the plot.

In this great task it is vital to recognise what we can and cannot do. We cannot make our children Christians—only God the Holy Spirit can do that work. But we can pray, live, teach and role-model discipleship in such a way that, in spite of our weakness and failings, we might lay a foundation for life and in God's goodness be a means of grace to our children.

Ephesians 6 v 4 is deceptively simple but comprehensive. Fathers are called to four things, one "negative", three "positive". We are to raise children:

1. In fairness: "do not provoke (or embitter) your children...". William Hendrickson observed that there were six ways to provoke (or embitter) your child. By over-protection, by favouritism, by discouragement, by trying to forge their God-given personality into a clone of yourself, by neglect and, finally, by bitter, harsh words.

Think about just one of those by way of example: favouritism. The patriarch Isaac favoured Esau while his wife Rebecca preferred Jacob and created a conflict that followed those boys well into their adulthood. In turn Jacob compounded the error by favouring Joseph, which in turn bred great jealousy of Joseph by his brothers. Resentment soon grows in a child who is constantly compared with siblings, and is often carried well into adult years. Our children need to know that we are on their side, that we love them unconditionally.

2. In tenderness: "but bring them up...". These are tender words that imply that we should nurture children with affection, care, time, encouragement, involvement and a listening ear. Bing Crosby's son committed suicide at the age of 51. He once told a reporter: "I never expected affection from my father so it didn't bother me". Perhaps it did more that he realised. Commentators say one reason Prince Charles was so grief-stricken at the death of the Queen Mother was because he heard from her two words that he rarely heard from his father: "Well done". Yes, even a Prince needs encouragement!

Masculine men should be tender, sympathetic, kind—especially towards their daughters, for whom they will provide an example of manhood that will go with them for life.

3. In firmness: "in the discipline and instruction..." This implies a systematic but spontaneous and natural training. Notice the two-fold emphasis in **Deuteronomy 6 v 4-9** on the "heart": "love the LORD your God with all your heart" (v 5), "these words ... shall be on your heart" (v 6). Notice also that it is fathers who are responsible to impress and apply God's wisdom to the everyday life of their children.

Today's culture is incredibly manipulative in its endeavours to shape and control our children's thinking, desires and behaviour. Our great aim is to get them to think Christianly, to sift and evaluate all that comes at them from the culture around through the grid of Christian truth. The Bible warns that foolishness (ie: anti

God, idolatry) is bound up in the heart of a child. So fathers, be realistic about and aware of the peer issues and pressures children face. Take the opportunities at every turn to apply gospel truth and thinking to everyday situations.

4. In Christ: "of the Lord". The focus is relational. The great ambition of the Christian father will be to point our children to the wisdom, beauty and righteousness of Christ, the great hero. Our goal and prayer must be to see our children grow into young adults who love Christ and love his wisdom.

It may be only eighteen words, but it represents a life-time's work to be obedient to the vision it presents!

4. The "being" of godly fatherhood

Start where you are. Every Christian father is surely aware of weaknesses and failings in parenting. You may feel yourself a miserable failure. The children are older and there is not much hope of redressing the situation. Or perhaps you are a "single parent" or a divorcee struggling with the pain of a broken marriage, the guilt and sense of failure that often pervades the ensuing relationships with the children.

The biblical counsel of hope and a fresh start is integral to the gospel. There may be huge bridges to rebuild in relationships but, wherever you are on the fathering scale, the start (or restart point) is our relationship with Christ. Here are five ways we can develop as Christian fathers:

1. Time with the Father: We have got to make our own relationship with the Lord the priority of our life. Everything else hangs off this. Nothing is more important. We must make time to develop our relationship with our heavenly Father (see chapter 2). Time in the Bible and prayer is the only thing that will focus me on what is true about God, myself, the world, the job that I do, my calling as a Christian. We will not get that perspective from anyone or anywhere else.

2. Rock and Role model: Our life is a letter. My own father adopted my two half sisters and myself amidst circumstances of deceit that would have caused many a man to desert. He was not a Christian but I thank God for him. For 25 years he modelled duty, sacrifice, dedication and grit. Every father, good or bad, Christian or not, provides a role model. Godly fathers have an immense influence not only on our own children but also, through them, upon the next generation as well. As believing fathers, our calling is to model a true Christian lifestyle. This will never be a perfect one, those closest to us will see us at our worst. And children will always see through hypocrisy and sham—but they will also recognise that we are struggling for honesty and integrity. We must first be ourselves what we want our children to be.

3. Relationship not religion: Our ambition is for our child to develop a relationship with God—not a religion about God. Godliness does not happen because a child is in the home of Christian parents. Real godliness is our goal—not just conforming to rules or a "Christian" lifestyle.

Every six months sit with your wife to discuss and set some goals. Plan an approach. A child has different needs at varying stages of life. Constantly ask yourself: Where is my child at? Where are they weak or struggling? What issues are bothering them or facing them at present? Think about how to encourage their personal reading of the Bible and prayer life. Pray with them. In addition to family prayers, (meal times are a great opportunity), encourage them to use some of the excellent Bible-reading material available these days. As fathers we must make the effort to read the Bible and pray with our children.

4. Make quality time: The sheer pace of life squeezes out best intentions but on our deathbed we will not be wishing that we had spent more time at work. Make and take the time for fatherhood. There is only one go at it. Being together, activities, fun, meals and talking are some of the best uses of your time.

Remember, *quality* time only comes when you spend *quantity* time with them.

5. Be accountable and be encouraged: Why not meet once a fortnight for an hour in a prayer triplet with other Christian fathers to study the Bible, pray and share issues? Perhaps someone who is a few years further down the track will give added insight and practical advice. Someone who will help encourage and challenge you to be a "Rock and Roler"—a rock of unwavering commitment to our wives and children, and a role model who knows that true success is to seek first the kingdom of God and his righteousness.

Real lives

Horace works as an IT programmer and is an elder in a local church.

After twelve years of fathering Horace feels there is no "golden technique" to be learned from all the books on the subject but tries to centre his approach on Paul's words on fathering in **1 Thessalonians 2**: "...encouraging, comforting and urging ... to live lives worthy of God" (NIV). Though Horace has a Christian mother, he did not come to Christ until his late twenties—so, in Christian development, he tries not to demand more of his children than he asked of himself at their age.

Struggling with the usual demands of a busy life, he and his wife aim to guard the hour before bedtime. Either of them will use this as a time to pray, read the Bible, encourage the children in their use of children's Bible notes, discuss issues arising in the day, attempting a balance of seriousness and fun.

What advice would he give new fathers? "Look after yourself physically, so that you can give energy as well as time!"

"Good enthusiastic Christian example, though obviously vital, is not enough in itself—you must also teach why you do things the way you do. Involve them in your Christian service wherever possible."

"Try not to demonise stuff on TV or in the culture but talk through the good and bad points of a programme or issue. Try to get them to think through life from a Christian mindset. Pick the big issues on which you will discipline, and be consistent—and always follow through your threats!"

Real lives

Dave is a self employed man in his 50s who went through a painful divorce before becoming a Christian 12 years ago.

The biggest practical problem he faced then as a Christian father was the loss of day-to-day contact with his young daughter and son. He made a point of maintaining a good relationship with his ex-wife in their common desire to care for the children. When at weekends he saw the children, he ensured they spent time relating to each other—not just enjoying outings etc—and that they had some gospel exposure at his church's Sunday School.

Contact in teenage years became more difficult when they moved abroad with their mother. However holiday times in England gave Dave the opportunity of extended times with both children. His advice on how best to influence children with the gospel in such a situation is: "Make it very clear where you stand, be the best father and Christian you can... and pray loads!"

Kevin, 42, is married to Karen and has two boys at home: Jason, 14, and Jonathan, 3. He drives a bus for a living.

Since becoming a Christian, Kevin has completely changed his whole view on his role as a father: "I can't think of a harder but more rewarding responsibility than being a Christian dad. It's been an amazing realisation that both the child and father share a Father in heaven. It has been a challenge knowing that I'm responsible for one of his children."

"It's also been a challenge trying to set an example and live right by God and walk in his ways before my all-seeing, all-hearing and all-repeating children! It may well be that God alone knows the minds and hearts of men, but my boy Johnny has a habit of telling everyone in daycare what I do."

DISCUSS

Q1. What do you most struggle with in yourself and the culture that directly affects your fathering?

Q2. What would you most like to be remembered for by your children and how are you going to seek to make that happen?

Q3. What ideas could you discuss with other men in your church about developing Christian fatherhood amidst the demands of work, church and family?

Q4. Discuss specific ways that you might be more faithful in prayer for your children.

BIBLE STUDY

Read Deuteronomy 6, one of the great Old Testament passages that directly touches upon fatherhood.

Q1. What is to characterise our relationship with God the Father according to verses 4 and 5?

Q2. How would such a relationship with God impact our approach to fathering?

Q3. What strikes you from verses 6 to 9 about the scope of this responsibility?

Q4. How might you work out these principles in practice, and what are the opportunities in your everyday family life to do so?

Q5. What is the greatest danger facing parents and children in a materialistic society and how are you to actively guard against it (see v 10-25)?

8 SERVANTS NOT PASSENGERS

Men and church

Hugh Palmer

Many men struggle to feel "at home" in church. Perhaps they have misunderstood what church is all about...

The gloom merchants of this world love a chapter title like this! It allows them to trot out all the latest statistics about how men are deserting the church; to dolefully recount the favourite grumbles about their particular church; to mutter clichés that suggest we live in a generation that has turned its back on institutions.

They may need reminding that they are reckoning without God. Worldwide, his church is growing not declining. Worst still, the western mindset may need reminding that our highly individualised society can mean we fail to hear the gospel properly. We can so personalise the gospel that we turn our back on God's plans!

In a one sentence snapshot of God's plans and purposes Paul writes this:

> For those whom [God] foreknew he also predestined to be conformed to the image of his Son, in order that he (Jesus) might be the firstborn among many brothers. **Romans 8 v 29**

Paul says that when God puts his hands on someone and calls them to himself, he does so in order that they might be godly (conformed to the image/likeness of his Son) and also that they might be part of his family (that Jesus might be the firstborn among many brothers). We talk of family planning in terms of limiting the size of our family, but God's planning works in the opposite direction. He wants Jesus to have many brothers. The gospel brings us to God, but it also brings us into God's family.

Family not Individuals

We may live in a generation that has turned its back on institutions, but we must not live as Christians who have turned their back on people—on God's people. Church is first and foremost people. When Peter makes his great gospel appeal at the end of the Day of Pentecost, and calls on the crowd to repent and be baptised, it is, in practice, a call to decide which community they are going to belong to. It is a call to remove their first loyalties from "this crooked generation" (**Acts 2 v 40**) and give them to the followers of Jesus to whom three thousand were added that day.

To speak of a generation that has turned its back on institutions easily becomes a cover for, in practice, turning our backs on people. When it's God's people we turn our backs on, then we discover we're running away from his gospel too. The last time someone on one of our evangelistic courses asked me the old question: "Do I have to go to church if I become a Christian?", I answered: "If you are a Christian, you are church, you are one of the family".

When Luke finishes his account of that early church on the Day of Pentecost, he does so by giving us a final paragraph which is a cameo portrait of a Christian community (**Acts 2 v 42**). Bible-centred: "They devoted themselves to the apostles' teaching". Practically, lovingly committed to each other: "...and fellowship". Cross-centred: "...to the breaking of bread" (more than just table fellowship, this almost certainly refers to the great remembrance sacrament of the Lord's Supper). With a dependence on God that makes it more than the sum of its parts: "...and the prayers". These are the distinctives that ought to be the first marks to look for in any church fellowship. We need to put our energies and encouragement into developing churches with these distinctives.

Servants not passengers

"It was he (Christ) who gave some to be apostles, some to be prophets, some to be evangelists, and some to be pastors and teachers, to prepare God's people for works of service, so that the body of Christ may be built up until we all reach unity in the faith and in the knowledge of the Son of God and become mature, attaining to the whole measure of the fullness of Christ". **Ephesians 4 v 11-13** (NIV)

Paul's idea of church does not encourage a dependency culture. This ministry of some (v 11) is there to produce a ministry of all (v 12). The pastor-teacher's job is to prepare God's people for works of service. A friend of mine makes the point very vividly on the back of his church card. It lists some of the responsibilities undertaken by individuals like treasurer, secretary, youth worker, but clearly states **"Ministers: all the congregation"**. To be Christian is to be one of God's people—to be one of God's people is to be in ministry! If that doesn't seem to fit with your current practice shock your pastor-teacher by asking him to put you to work!

Of course, for others the danger is not a dependency culture but an immature independence. That is not the picture that is painted here either. Just as the church involves every member ministry, so its aim is every member maturity. The relational model for the church is neither dependency nor independency, but interdependence. A couple of verses later, Paul goes on to speak of "truthing in love" and pictures the church as a "body, joined and held together by every supporting ligament growing and building itself up in love as each part does its work".

Interdependence does not come easy to selfish natures. That's why so much of the New Testament is written to help Christians relate in a godly way to each other. That's why there is this constant refrain urging us to love and forgive one another. Not in some weak, limp way—for we're also urged to encourage and teach and admonish one another. To reduce Christian fellowship to having a cup of coffee with someone is to suck the life out of it. We should not be able to avoid the messy involvement of family life. Men have a track record of doing just that in society. We Christian men need to be modelling this firm concern for one another in the church family so that it can be recovered in other family life too.

Missionaries not couch potatoes

One of the difficulties for many men about this kind of church talk is that it is very **relational**, and they can be very **goal orientated**. Too often we emphasise one at the expense of the other. Yet, a church without a goal has lost sight of the plot.

A church without mission at its heart has lost the heart of the God who brought it into being. That early church in Acts chapter 2 had a magnetic attraction. They enjoyed "favour with all the people. And the Lord added to their number day by day those who were being saved" **Acts 2 v 47**. If godly, relational living is meant to give it that quality, then it needs too those ready to give a reason for the hope that is in them.

The church is to be an open circle, not just a closed clique—but an open circle that can explain the life and vitality that it enjoys. Later on it took persecution to turn this church into a missionary force (**Acts 8 v 1, 4**). Notice that all the leaders got left behind so that it was ordinary Christian men and women who were spreading the message. The magnet and the missionary are constant expressions of God's mission... through his church.

To turn from a couch potato into a missionary need not be a long journey. If I can't learn the message from one of countless courses or books, I can always bring a friend to someone who knows how to tell it. Basically, it's a question of heartbeat. If there is a love for the lost, and a genuine concern for Jesus' name and reputation, then no man can let the church turn into a closed circle.

DISCUSS

Q1. How do you balance work, home, leisure and church responsibilities?

Q2. How can you encourage others to have those accountable friendships which will build each other up in their Christian lives?

Q3. "I don't want to start talking for Jesus until I know the answers. There's nothing worse than making him look a fool because of my ignorance." If I'd followed my own advice, I would never have opened my mouth. What would you say to me, a defensive new convert trying to justify his silence?

BIBLE STUDY

1 Peter 2 v 4-12

Q1. What encouragement do you discover for "unimpressive" churches in verses 4-8?

Q2. Who is in a position to tell of God's actions and how does that affect what we say (verses 9 and 10)?

Q3. What are the tensions, and the hopes and fears, Peter has for Christians relating to the world around them (verses 11 and 12)?

9 WORK THE WORK OF HIM...

Men and work

Tim Thornborough

I owe, I owe, so off to work I go... Is work a matter of drudgery, or should we find joy in it as Christians? And what is the place of witness at work?

John turns off his computer at the end of another long, hard day. "Another day over," he thinks to himself as he walks home, "now I can get on with my real life".

Geoff is sitting at the wheel of his bus stuck in traffic, breathing in the heat and fumes, and dreading the next stop where he will have to deal with a crowd of rowdy and excited schoolkids. "Oh God, get me out of here," he prays.

Brian glances at his watch, and realises to his horror that it is past 8pm. As he dashes for the door, he is already imagining the argument he will be having with his wife when he gets home. He hasn't seen his children for days. "Still, I've had a fantastic day," he thinks, "I love this job".

Many Christian men have a curiously divided view of work. Is it simply the means by which I put bread on the table, or generate sufficient funds for holidays? Is it right that I "fulfil my potential" and have a career path that brings me to the top? If I find my job tedious, dull or tiresome, is that a sign that I should move on?

Is it simply a convenient place to meet pagans and share Jesus with them (and get paid in the process)?

We often get bogged down with the more obvious issues, like business ethics and the demands of time, family, responsibilities and money, without resolving the underlying principles that the Bible lays out for why we should work. The answers may surprise you.

God—the worker

The Bible opens with a glorious picture of a God who loves to work. He takes pleasure in forming and crafting the universe we now live in. He delights in his creative acts, and enjoys standing back and nodding contentedly at the brilliance of what he has done. And he took no greater pleasure than in the creation of humankind: "And God saw everything that he had made, and behold, it was very good" (**Genesis 1 v 31**).

Man—the worker

It is not surprising therefore that the first Adam (the name means "man"), who was made in God's image, was also a worker by nature. Man was commanded to: "Be fruitful and multiply and fill the earth and subdue it..."; and he was placed in the garden to "work it and keep it" (**Genesis 1 v 28; 2 v 15**). His job, in short, was to be productive in the world—to use it creatively and care for it as God's representative. This is the reason that work is enjoyable to many people. The satisfaction of a job well done. The pleasure in making something. The sense of wellbeing that we have done something well. But that is not the end of the story...

Man—the fallen worker

But mankind fell from this position of responsibility and grace by foolishly disobeying God—by disobeying his single loving command. It is interesting to note that the consequences of the Fall on the man and woman are directly related to their roles in the created order. Eve was to be the means of fruitful multiplication of mankind, but now she must give birth in pain and danger. Adam was to work and care for the world, but now the ground he must till is cursed with thorns and weeds, and "by the sweat of your face you shall eat bread, till you return to the ground...". Joy in work has been replaced by frustration, toil and a sense of meaninglessness, as Solomon was to write later:

> What has a man from all the toil and striving of heart with which he toils beneath the sun? For all his days are full of sorrow, and his work is a vexation. Even in the night his heart does not rest. This also is vanity.

Ecclesiastes 2 v 22-23

This, at root, is the reason why work is a frustration for many: boring, difficult and stressful. But this is compounded by the effects of sin within ourselves and those who employ us. Sinful mankind is no longer constrained to care for the world or for each other, and so the workplace can easily become a system of exploitation and greed, where people are seen as a commodity to be used and then thrown away when they no longer function efficiently.

Christ—the new Adam

But the destruction that Adam's sin brought to mankind has been overturned by the new Adam—the Lord Jesus Christ. Just like his Father, he too is a worker. But he did not just wield the tools of a carpenter, but came to carry out a greater work. He worked the work of God in his ministry of teaching, healing and proclamation, which culminated in his death upon the cross. This was the work that won forgiveness and new life for us.

Christians—renewed workers

In Christ, we experience something of the new order that Christ has brought into the world, but we are still plagued by the old order of sin and futility. We can expect that work will continue to be a curious mix of enjoyment and grind, satisfaction and frustration. But we also have a new set of values which put work in its place. Just as our nationality becomes secondary to being part of the kingdom of God, so our work becomes part of the bigger picture of what God is doing in the world, and our part in it. Work for the believer represents an opportunity to serve others and fulfill our responsibilities to family and the people of God, as well as a fruitful place to engage with others for the sake of the gospel. Love is the great motivation for Christian living, so here are five loving reasons why we should get out of bed in the morning.

Love—the reason for work

1. So that we should not be a burden on others

> For you yourselves know how you ought to imitate us, because we were not idle when we were with you, nor did we eat anyone's bread without paying for it, but with toil and labour we worked night and day, that we might not be a burden to any of you.
>
> **2 Thessalonians 3 v 7-8**

Paul says that one big reason for work is not to burden others. In other words, that we pull our own weight. This is obviously the loving thing to do. If we are lazy or idle, then others will bear the burden for us. Men in particular are called to be self-sacrificial in our love for others, as Christ was. We should therefore be prepared to "go the extra mile."

2. To serve the community

Galatians 6 v 10 tells us that "as we have opportunity, let us do good to everyone…". We are to be like our heavenly Father who sends rain on both the good and the bad. Even such mindless jobs as turning around the "Stop/Go" signs at a roadworks have a beneficial value to others: it is keeping people safe, while improving the environment. It is sometimes hard to find the connection between our actual job and the benefit to the community, but it is worth searching for to give us the correct motivation for working at what may be a mundane or repetitive task. If, on reflection, your job provides no service to the community, or else it is a burden on others, it may be worth considering if you are in the right job!

3. To provide for family and relatives

Honour widows who are truly widows. But if a widow has children or grandchildren, let them first learn to show godliness to their own household and to make some return to their parents, for this is pleasing in the sight of God.

1 Timothy 5 v 3-4

The traditional role of man as the prime breadwinner has changed significantly in our society over the last 50 years, but the responsibility to provide remains. And not just for our own family, but also for the extended family. Honouring our parents does not stop when we leave home.

4. So that we have something to share with those in need

Let the thief no longer steal, but rather let him labour, doing honest work with his own hands, so that he may have something to share with anyone in need.

Ephesians 4 v 28

We are all called to be generous, because we have been the recipients of God's immense generosity to us in the gospel. It is easy to fall into thinking that we have worked for what we earn, and therefore we can spend it on ourselves. On the contrary, all that we have comes from God, and it pleases him when we are generous to the poor and needy, especially those of the household of faith.

5. To support gospel workers

I thank my God in all my remembrance of you, always in every prayer of mine for you all making my prayer with joy, because of your partnership in the gospel from the first day until now.

Philippians 1 v 3-5

When Paul says "partnership" he means more than money—he includes prayer, encouragement and other forms of practical help. Giving to the work of God is our responsibility and it should also be our joy. We should welcome opportunities to give to God's work, knowing that gospel work has an eternal significance that stretches way beyond the value of our own work. For the man of God, working to give to the work of the gospel should be a powerful encouragement to keep at it. Some people work overtime in order to give, others work on after retirement in order to be able to give to the work of God. It is a loving and godly thing to do.

The world-weary, fallen attitude to work could be summed up in the car sticker which says: "I owe, I owe, so off to work I go". For God's redeemed humanity, our motivation should be entirely different. We work, not simply because we must, but because it pleases our heavenly Father, and is the loving thing to do. Perhaps our motto should be: "I love, I love, so off to work I shove"!

Workers as gospel workers

The other major significance of work for believers is that it is the place where we have regular contact with non Christians—and therefore a fruitful place for gospelling.

Many men feel awkward about this, and feel unable to be public about their faith in Christ in their workplace. We certainly need all the encouragement we can get to be appropriately Christian at work. Some important things to take note of:

1. **Plant a flag as early as you can:** The longer you delay letting people know you are a believer, the harder it is. Work is not the place to stand on a soap box, but visual clues often lead to opportunities to let it be known you are a Christian. A badge, or a Bible verse on your desk, or as a screen saver on your computer, can be sufficient to prompt questions from others. Learning to be relaxed and open in conversation, without pressing it too hard, is also helpful. Talk openly about being in church at the weekend,

or the Christian holiday or camp you have been on. People are much more accepting of our beliefs than we think (until, of course, we start to suggest that they should believe too!).

2. Be holy: Taking liberties with time, gossip, sloppy work and irritability will annoy others and discredit your witness. Honesty, faithfulness, good humour and integrity will make the gospel attractive (**Titus 2 v 10**).

3. Be ethical: You may be asked from time to time to do something that you think is unethical. Let's be clear. Our first responsibility is to our heavenly Father, not to our human employers. We need to be firm and clear about not being involved in any dodgy dealing; even if it puts our job under threat. "He who honours me, I also will honour says the Lord" (**1 Samuel 2 v 30**).

4. Use opportunities as they arise: There are many formal and informal opportunities to bring work colleagues under the sound of the gospel. You may have a lunch-time meeting that you can attend at a local church. Many more of these meetings are springing up, which offer a good mix of Bible-teaching and encouragement for Christians, and thoughtful evangelism for others. Try and find a local meeting that you could start supporting and using. Some have even been able to start a small fellowship group at work, and to run occasional evangelistic events.

Informal opportunities are many and varied: whether it's to make a Christian comment on the news of the day, to offer to pray for someone, or to share your testimony or the gospel with someone. Like good boy scouts we should always be prepared! (See **1 Peter 3 v 15**.)

BIBLE STUDY

Read Colossians 3 v 22 – 4 v 1

Q1. What should be our attitude at work (v 22-23)?
How can we help ourselves to keep this in mind?
How could this bring us into conflict with our earthly
masters?

Q2. What should the chief motivation be for working hard
(v 24)? Why should this make us good workers?

Q3. (4 v 1) What should be our main attitude towards
those who work under us? Apart from fair wages,
what else should this command lead us to do?

Read 1 Peter 3 v 15

Q4. "Reverence for Christ" is the first base for evangelism.
How can you demonstrate that quality better at
work?

Q5. Are you ready to answer their questions? If not, how
can you make yourself ready?

DISCUSS

Q1. Do you love your work or hate it? Can you trace your feelings about work to any aspect of our "createdness" or our "falsenness"?

Q2. "Love is the Christian motive for work". Talk honestly about the way you currently think about your work. Go through the five loving reasons to work in the article, and work out which are most appropriate to you. Do you think it is realistic to think of work in this way?

Q3. "Use opportunities as they arise". Talk about some of the recent opportunities you have had to share something of the gospel with others at work. Did they go well or badly? What would encourage you to be more vocal or demonstrative about your Christian faith at work?

Q4. What issues for your personal holiness, or ethical issues do you face at work? How can you be encouraged to deal with them better?

10 WHY AND HOW

Men and witness

Rico Tice

What should our motivation be for spreading the good news about Jesus? And exactly how should we go about it?

There are four things the devil does not want you to do as he prowls around like a roaring lion (**1 Peter 5 verse 8**).

He doesn't want you to read the Bible—so that God won't speak to you.

He doesn't want you to pray—so that you can't speak to God.

He doesn't want you to go to church—so that you won't hear God, speak to God, or encourage and be encouraged by others.

But, if the devil can't stop you doing these things, then **he doesn't want you telling others.** He doesn't want you giving yourself to the "ministry of reconciliation" (**2 Corinthians 5 v 18**). He doesn't want you to be one of Christ's ambassadors.

Evangelism—spreading the good news that Jesus Christ is Lord—is therefore inherently difficult, and always a spiritual battle. After all, the very purpose of it is to raid the devil's kingdom and rescue those under his thumb. Now, in order to keep the motivation high for witness, let me put before you the four "G's". May these keep you going as you seek to dig up the motivation to keep at the glorious task of reconciliation. The "G's' are: Grace; Gehenna; Glory; Godliness. Let's take them one at a time...

Grace

Paul writes in **2 Corinthians 4 v 1**:

> Therefore, since through God's mercy we have this ministry, we do
> not lose heart.

In this passage he marvels at the way the Christian is only a Christian because God has had mercy on him. So the fact that I can see who Jesus is, that I recognise Jesus as my master, is a miracle. It is because God sent his Holy Spirit to open my blind eyes and transform my heart. It was his Holy Spirit who enabled me to see "God's glory in the face of Christ" **(2 Corinthians 4 v 6)**—that Jesus was God. And it means that my heart should always be overwhelmed with thanksgiving at God's mercy for the privilege of being Christian and **(2 Corinthians 4 v 5)** preaching Christ to others. We do not deserve it. I love what Bishop Alf Stanway said to some men entering the ministry in Pittsburgh, USA. It sums up the motivation of grace: "If other people knew you like God knows you—all your faults, all your vain thoughts, all your sins, all the things in your heart, all the wrong thoughts you ever had—would they trust you with the kind of work God trusts you with? Here is the supreme confidence God has in his own grace. He'll take the likes of you and me and give you the privilege of being his saints."

Gehenna

"Gehenna" was the name of the fiery rubbish dump outside Jerusalem that the Lord Jesus famously used as an illustration of hell. And it is the reality of hell, and our responsibility to warn men and women of this clear and present danger, that should spur us on to witnessing. **Ezekiel 3 v 16-18** are striking verses which seem to be much neglected in Christian thinking today:

> At the end of seven days the word of the LORD came to me: "Son of
> man, I have made you a watchman for the house of Israel. Whenever
> you hear a word from my mouth, you shall give them warning from
> me. If I say to the wicked [and wickedness in the Bible is most often
> defined as those who live without reference to God], 'You shall sure-

> ly die,' and you give him no warning, nor speak to warn the wicked
> from his wicked way, in order to save his life, that wicked person
> shall die for his iniquity, but his blood I will require at your hand."

And if we do not tell people or warn them about hell, then we are nothing like Jesus Christ, who warns people again and again and again in the most stark terms:

> I tell you, my friends, do not fear those who kill the body, and after
> that have nothing more that they can do. But I will warn you whom
> to fear: fear him who, after he has killed, has authority to cast into
> hell.

Luke 12 v 4-5

And whatever else you do for people—if you do not warn them—on Judgement Day they will not thank you.

It is most striking that in the light of the awful reality of Gehenna (hell), Bishop Frank Retief in Cape Town asks his clergy to organise their diaries around the following Mission Statement: "People without Christ go to hell". He says to his clergy: "Please organise your time around that truth". Do you?

The Bible does speak of eternal torment for those who died having ignored the rescue of the cross, as they pay for their sin themselves, and this should be a huge motivation for witness. As J.I. Packer has written: "Hell is not the product of human speculation. An endless hell can no more be removed from the New Testament than can an endless heaven".

Glory

The glory of something is its intrinsic worth, value or splendour. The glory of a sunset is its beauty, of a craftsman his skill, and of a lion its strength; and the glory of God lies in his character of holiness and love, wisdom and power.

But there should be a right jealousy for God's name. A deep desire that men and women treat God as God. We want the God we adore to be adored by others. I recently got married and I am surprised by my desire to make sure others see the qualities I so cherish in my wife. I so enjoy them that I long for others to recognise them, and I am actually hurt if others don't give her her right worth.

Godliness

Godliness is obviously all about being like God. And right at the heart of being like God is having a concern for the lost. I love the words of John Chapman, an evangelist from Sydney: "You cannot be godly, you cannot be godly and not be concerned for the lost. God was so concerned for the lost that he sent his Son to die".

So if we are concerned to be like God, then we must not separate godliness from evangelism, as sadly many do. Many think they are godly, committed Christians, yet witnessing to others is given no time in their diaries. I love the way we see God's heart laid bare in **Luke 15**. In all three parables something of great value goes missing—a sheep, a coin, a son. On each occasion an all-out search is made for the lost item. The shepherd goes after the sheep until he finds it (v 4). The woman sweeps the house and searches till she finds the coin (v 8). The father's eyes are scanning the horizon for his son (v 20). And we matter so much to God that he sent his Son, our shepherd, to search us out and do whatever it takes to bring us back to the Father, even dying on a cross.

And then in all three parables we see the heart of God is exposed, as finding that which was lost merits a great celebration. I think you can probably empathize with that if you just remember the relief you have felt when having lost something that was precious to you—your diary, phone, wallet or even your parents when you were a child.

The sense of relief and joy to be reunited is enormous. **Luke 15 v 7** tells me that there was rejoicing right across heaven on the day I came home to my Father. This is emphasized further in verse 10 where Jesus says there is a party in heaven when one person repents. And this means that to be godly, as Bill Hybels writes: "We never lock eyes with someone who does not matter to God, who does not warrant an all-out search and for whom the whole of heaven would not rejoice if they were to bow down and confess Christ as Lord".

Well, if that is **why** we witness to men—Grace, Gehenna, Glory, Godliness—the next question is **how**? I think a five-letter pneumonic TRUST contains five keys to building authentic "witnessing" relationships with men: Time; Reality; Understanding; Sacrifice; Tell.

Time

Remember Bishop Frank Retief's words to his clergy: "Organise your diaries around the fact people without Christ go to hell". And there is so often no other way to win people's trust than by giving them our most precious commodity—time.

In London I often think love is a four-letter word: **time**. Before ordination I used to work at *Hewlett Packard*, a computer company, and I can so clearly remember the change in a relationship with a colleague when we played golf together at the weekend. He knew then that I really wanted to know him because I had given up my own time, not office time, to be with him. I think a useful tip here is to tithe your time (give ten percent) to witness. Perhaps one lunch in ten or one weekend in ten is given to quality time with non-Christian friends. But the key is to block out time, block out the diary. Spending time shows that we care. As Bill Hybels has written: "They don't care how much you know till they know how much you care".

Reality

The apostle Paul lamented his own life in **Romans 7 v 19**: "For I do not do the good I want, but the evil I do not want is what I keep on doing."

The non-Christian often looks at the Christian man and thinks: "This is not possible, I could never be a Christian". And they need to see our struggles, our battles, and our dependence on God's grace.

Understanding

What is life like for this man? What are his struggles? The key to understanding is asking questions. For example, who are the most important people in this man's life? And spiritually the question I love to ask is: If they died tonight and God said, "Why should I let you into heaven?", what would be their reply?

Sacrifice

We show our friends that we love them enough to make sacrifices for them. This may mean in the workplace helping them out with a project but not taking the credit; staying late to help them solve a problem. And it may have real implications in terms of time and finance outside the workplace in the home. But the issue is where is this person really needing some help and how can I give it in a way that is unselfconscious and just part of being a friend?

Tell

Pray your friends will grow spiritually hungry, and pray for courage and an opportunity to explain what lies at the very heart of your life.

A great way to frame your story is to work out when you understood the **identity**, **mission** and **call** of Jesus. So when did you see who Jesus was; when did you see why he came; and when did you see what it means to follow him? Whether you are from a Christian or non-Christian home, these three themes go right to the heart of the gospel's work in your life, and it keeps your testimony absolutely Christ-focused. Then we just have to do our bit, which is to preach Christ, **2 Corinthians 4 v 5**, and pray that God will do the miracle and open blind eyes to Jesus, **2 Corinthians 4 v 6**.

Bruce is a senior manager for a credit card company.

His evangelism is focussed on a small group of close friends from school, college and time spent abroad.

"I don't make new friendships quickly but tend to stick with a smaller number of really good friends. I aim to invite them to church and speak to them regularly about the gospel but within the context of a genuine friendship. I have found that if we spend time together, opportunities naturally crop up—after all my faith is a major part of my life so it would be strange not to talk about it."

Drinks after work or dinner parties are good places to meet and chat but Bruce believes it is important to meet people one to one too without the pressure of a group. "I have a mental list of five or six good friends and I try to meet them as often as I can for dinner or a coffee—anywhere we can have a deeper conversation than we might in a pub with the boys. Weekends away and holidays are also great opportunities to share your faith with friends—it's not always necessary to plan opportunities, just be ready to take them!"

Bruce also emphasises the importance of prayer in evangelism. "I know that nothing will happen without God's help, so I pray for good conversation which will stimulate interest and that I will explain my faith in an honest and gentle way. Ultimately I know that all I have to do is be there for my friends, sharing my faith and living it out, and trust that God will carry out his plans".

Real lives

Keith, 57, is a taxi driver. His anti-social working hours mean that most of his opportunities for evangelism come up at work.

"I'm on the road by 3am and back finished by 1pm. I'm usually in bed by 9pm. This routine is not ideal socially for making new friends and talking to them about Jesus. I occasionally meet people walking the dog in the park in the afternoon," he says.

But the real opportunities to talk come in the cab. "People like to chat in the cab and with all the traffic jams there is often time to talk in some depth. It happens more often now that I pray for opportunities! I find myself talking freely about the love of God and the peace of Jesus to my passengers. I think the next move is to have some leaflets to give out, and maybe details of London churches where they can go to lunchtime services to hear the gospel."

DISCUSS

Q1. The four "G"s are Grace, Gehenna, Glory and Godliness. Which of these motives most moves you? Why?

Q2. Go through each of the TRUST headings in the "How to" section (Time, Reality, Understanding, Sacrifice, Hell). Share any encouragements you have had with each of them, and talk over how you can encourage each other to improve on them.

Q3. If someone asked you: "Why are you a Christian?" what would your answer be? Practice talking about your own experience of Christ: use Rico's *identity*, *mission* and *call* model if you can to frame your own story of how you became a Christian.

Q4. List three people you would like to see come to Christ. What would you say to them if you had the opportunity? Spend some time praying for them, and for the courage to speak to them or invite them to something.

BIBLE STUDY

Read 2 Corinthians 4 v 1-7

Q1. Who has given us the job of spreading the good news (v 1)?

Q2. It is God's gospel, and he alone can convert people—so why is v 2 important? In what ways are we tempted to do the things v 2 warns against? And what does that show?

Q3. Why do people not understand the gospel (v 3-4)? So what is required to bring people to him?

Q4. What is the only message that we should give to people (v 5)? Again—why are we tempted to substitute "other gospels" for the one true gospel? Why is this ultimately a waste of time?

11 POURING WATER INTO BOTTLES

Men and discipling

William Taylor

Mentoring... discipling... personal evangelism. They're all off-putting words to describe a basic skill we all need to develop. Sharing our faith one to one...

The purpose of this chapter is to explain how to work individually both with non-Christian and Christian men. We are not speaking here about the informal personal encouragement that should be a normal part of every Christian man's ministry to other believers (**Colossians 3 v 16**). Rather we are concerned with a more formal, planned, regular meeting of men for study of God's word, prayer and encouragement.

This sort of work can take place as a Christian man meets with a non-Christian seeking to "teach Christ" to that individual. It can also take place as an older Christian instructs a younger Christian in the basics of the Christian life and Christian ministry.

The aim of "one-to-one", or "personal" work is the same as in any Christian ministry. We work with men individually in order to present men "mature in Christ" (**Colossians 1 v 28**).

However, in a one-to-one relationship there is a difference. For in a one-to-one relationship there is far greater opportunity to deal with individual issues and concerns of discipleship. One famous Christian leader once memorably put it like this: "Giving a talk, it is said, is like throwing water from a bucket over a row of bottles; a few drops may enter some. Speaking to individuals, on the other hand, is like pouring water from a jug into the narrow neck of each bottle".

Certainly that has been my experience. As one who has both engaged in personal ministry of this sort, and been on the receiving end of it, I can testify to its unique effectiveness in nurturing and leading a person to maturity.

The resources for "one-to-one" ministry are no different to any other ministry that brings about Christian growth. The Bible, a prayerful dependence on God to do his work by his Spirit and a loving concern for individual members of God's family are all that is needed. God tells us that *new birth* into his family comes by his Spirit through his word. God tells us that *growth* within his family comes about by his Spirit through his word.

New Birth: In **John 3 v 5** Jesus tells Nicodemus that a person cannot enter the kingdom unless they are born of water and the Spirit. He re-affirms our utter dependence upon him to give us new life in **John 6 v 63**. But in v 63 Jesus makes it plain that God does this work of bringing new life to the spiritually dead by his Spirit through his word. "The flesh is of no avail," he says, meaning that we cannot help ourselves in this matter. Too right! A dead person cannot bring themself to life! So it is the Spirit who gives life. But Jesus immediately goes on to make plain that: "The words that I have spoken to you are spirit and life". So new birth comes to a person by God's Spirit through God's word. This point is confirmed for us over and again in the New Testament. In **1 Peter 1 v 23** Peter explains that his readers have been born again "through the living and abiding word of God". In **James 1 v 18** James tells us that we have been "brought forth by the word of truth". It is the gospel word of Christ that is God's power for salvation. This personal ministry of one-to-one Bible reading with a non-Christian is a wonderful way of exposing them to the word of life.

Growth: In **John 15 v 1-8** Jesus uses the picture language of the vine and explains that it is through his indwelling words, and through prayer shaped by his word, that true Christian growth and fruitfulness comes. Peter speaks of the same idea in **1 Peter 2 v 2** as he uses the picture language of the new-born baby craving spiritual milk (or wordy milk) so that we may grow up to salvation. It is by his Spirit through his word that God brings us to maturity in Christ. And Paul emphasises the same idea in Ephesians as he tells us that the word gifts of teaching and evangelism have been given to the church to enable works of ministry so that we grow up into Christ and are no longer children, tossed to and fro by the waves and carried about by every wind of doctrine (**Ephesians 4 v 11–16**).

So the resources needed for one-to-one ministry with individuals are really very simple. A Bible, a prayerful dependence on God to do his work by his Holy Spirit, and a loving concern for individuals are all that is needed. R.A. Torrey, one of the great personal workers of the last century, has this to say about personal work: "Let your reliance be wholly in the Spirit of God and in the word of God". I had the great privilege of being on the receiving end of one-to-one personal work with Mark Ruston (former vicar of The Round Church in Cambridge). I once heard him giving a talk on the subject and one of his most memorable pieces of advice was: "Pray before, pray during, pray afterwards".

Principles applied

Method: the danger of speaking about any particular "method" is that it might reduce what is essentially a relational exercise to mere mechanics. One-to-one work must flow out of a loving concern for the individual as we seek to encourage and nurture a Christian brother or lead an unbeliever to faith. Make sure that, alongside a regular meeting to study, there is also plenty of opportunity for a relationship to develop with the person with whom you are working. This may simply be a matter of regular contact in an office or a home setting. Alternatively, we may arrange to go out for a drink together, meet for lunch, play sport, or some other activity.

However, assuming that this is in place, there are basically four elements to the time we spend together:

Sharing of news and chat: A good period of time at the start of our meeting to catch up with one another's news.

Bible study: The central part of our time will be given over to study and prayer. I tend to prepare a short, simple study with a very few leading questions on the passage. I like to work through a book of the Bible passage by passage. As far as is possible, I try to do a "model study" of the passage so that together we are both learning the lessons of the passage—and at the same time I am teaching him how to read the Bible for himself. Doing this also helps to guard him against those who use the Bible wrongly.

Prayer: Before the study we always pray that God would speak to us by his Spirit through his word. I will pray even with a non-Christian. Short prayers that they would easily be able to copy later on if they come to faith or as they start to pray themselves. After the study we tend to pray about the things we have learned and about any other issues that are going on in the individual's life.

Specific aspects of discipleship: I try to make sure that there is additional time to discuss issues arising either from the passage studied or from general conversation before or after the study. Frequently there will be some aspect of being a Christian that the person wants to talk through. In addition I keep a mental list of the kind of things that any young Christian ought to be putting into practice and try to make sure the majority of them are covered over the time that we meet together. Things like: Can he explain the gospel simply to a friend or colleague? Can he give his own personal testimony? Does he know how to have a personal time of Bible study and prayer? Is he beginning to bring his discipleship into his family life? Has he got a good home church and fellowship group to go to? Is he serving? Has he sorted out his giving? ... and so on. Many of these issues will come up quite naturally as we study the Bible together.

Materials

One of the questions people always ask me when we are talking about beginning this sort of one-to-one work is: What should I study? Given that God does is work of bringing someone to new life, or growing them, by his Spirit through his word, the most important thing is that we study the Bible together.

With a non-Christian: I always try to study a Gospel. Usually I study John's Gospel because it's the Gospel I know best. We usually study a chapter at a time.

With a Christian: There are a number of quite useful pre-packaged materials for study which you may choose to work through together. You will find some excellent examples on the Good Book Company website (see page 128), some of the specifically designed for one-to-one work. There are studies that will take you through a book of the Bible, and others that will take a topical theme and study it in-depth from several parts of the Bible over a few weeks.

Personally I prefer to study a book of the Bible for the reasons outlined above. What we study will depend on the level of maturity of the individual. With new Christians, I will often study either John's Gospel or a letter like Colossians or Romans. With an older Christian who ought to be thinking about ministry for himself, I will usually study 2 Timothy so that we can learn those key lessons on Christian ministry.

Key Tips

Never meet one-to-one like this with a person of the opposite sex (unless you're married to them!).

Getting started: Perhaps the most difficult thing is to get started. Be pro-active in seeking out people to work one-to-one with. Work with people who are hungry to learn. My aim as I try to reach non-Christians is always eventually to get them into a one-to-one learning relationship. Once you feel you know someone well enough, be bold in asking them. I will always give them an easy escape route so that they can say "No" if they don't want to meet up.

Getting Ready: Mark Ruston's advice again: "Pray before, pray during, pray after". Make sure both you and he have read the passage before you meet. Prepare a maximum of three or four simple questions from the passage. The aim is for you to learn together and to study together in a simple, informal way.

Where to meet: You need to think carefully about where you are going to meet. Make sure that it isn't somewhere where the person you are meeting with will be embarrassed. One person told me that they had met one-to-one in a public open-plan office for several months! However, a private office or home aren't bad places to meet. Lots of our one-to-one work takes place in *Starbucks*!

The Meeting: Keep to time. I find an hour is quite enough. Much better to leave them wanting more than have them wishing there was less! Get all the little details sorted out before you start. No telephone interruptions. The kettle already boiled before they come so as not to waste time. Two Bibles in the same translation ready to use. I even try to make sure that I can see the clock so that it isn't too obvious that I need to keep a rough eye on the time!

How often and for how many months: I try to meet each week, but invariably it ends up being more like two or three times a month. Usually I let the person know before we start that I would expect to meet with him for six months to a year. But those things are flexible and if we're making great progress, and he is still keen to go on and seems to have a lot to learn, then we'll go on longer.

Conclusion: One-to-one ministry is immensely valuable and enormously rewarding. It is also one of the most under-rated ministries in the church today. As I look around our own church it is often evident who the people are who have had someone spend time with them like this. Jesus tells us to: "Follow me and I will make you fishers of men". One-to-one ministry is a huge help to those who are wanting to follow Christ. Frequently we find those we spend time with growing in their own usefulness in ministry.

Real lives

James is 31 and works as a fundraiser for a London charity.

He's been a Christian since he was 17, but it is only in the last few years that he feels his faith has really started to flourish. "When I moved to London I joined a church that was really serious about teaching the Bible. I joined a Bible-study group and before long was asked whether I would like to read with a guy called William. This was a new concept for me, and to be honest I had no idea what to expect so I suppose I was a bit apprehensive, especially as this guy seemed so much more godly than me!"

James arranged to meet with William every Thursday morning before work and they started going through 2 Timothy together. "I had never read the Bible so thoroughly before and I was amazed at the way it related directly to my life. We went through the book in some detail and I learnt a huge amount about how to read and apply the Bible. We also chatted about life in general and prayed about things that were happening to us. I became really excited about reading the Bible and I was encouraged to sort out my own prayer life and quiet times."

Perhaps most of all though, James valued the time that William set aside to read with him. "I was struck by the fact that this busy man with so many demands on his time would put aside an hour a week to read with someone like me. It was a great privilege and taught me how important one-to-one discipleship is, not just in understanding the Bible but for encouragement."

James read with William for a year and now meets with other guys who read with him. "I enjoy working through a book of the Bible week by week with someone else. It's also a great way of being accountable to somebody and getting to know them on a deeper level."

One to One: Peter and Terry

Five years ago, after attending a men's supper evening, Peter started meeting with Terry after work late on a Friday afternoon once a fortnight.

After a few months looking at the gospel through John Stott's book *Basic Christianity* Peter, from a Roman Catholic background, came to faith in Christ. Since then the two men have continued to meet fortnightly for an hour late on Friday afternoon.

In that time they have used a number of different Bible Study guides in the Old and New Testament as well as *Disciplines of a Godly Man* and *Finishing Strong*. Both are amazed at the breadth of things they have been able to cover through this hour together and Peter is now serving in the leadership of his local church. "Studying the Bible, praying together and being encouraged like this has grown me as a Christian like nothing else," says Peter.

DISCUSS

Q1. What benefit do you think you might gain from meeting one-to-one with another man to read, encourage and pray?

Q2. Can you think of any younger Christian who might value your experience, guidance or knowledge? What steps could you take to start meeting with them?

Q3. Some churches set up a more formal prayer partner, or Bible-reading partnership scheme. How useful would it be to start such a scheme in your church? How would you go about it?

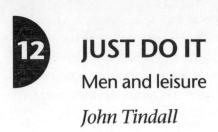

JUST DO IT

Men and leisure

John Tindall

Never have there been so many opportunities for leisure. But in our workaholic, high-pressure culture, men are often dogged by a sense of guilt about relaxing...

Reverend George Strong spends every Thursday afternoon on the squash courts owned by the Protectional Insurance Company, whose offices are close to the church where he works. He safeguards those two hours like nothing else in his ministry. He invites selected members of his church to join him as long as they're fit enough to survive and don't humiliate him on the court. When the assistant minister pulls his leg about this activity, he mutters something about "evangelism". Is this pastor acting remotely biblically in his passion, and in lamely justifying it on the grounds that it's an extension to his work?

Confusion

Provisions for leisure for the quality of life are as important as those for health and education. Governments should ensure their citizens a variety of accessible leisure and recreational opportunities of the highest quality.[1]

As for leisure, the church has never been able to make up its mind about it. The Bible says little about it directly. Christians through the centuries have also said and thought little about it, preferring to feel guilty about time spent in leisure.[2]

Taking those two quotations at face value would lead you to conclude that the secular world knows exactly where it stands on the importance of leisure—and that the Bible and the Christian church are unsure what to think. For sure, you won't find soccer in Solomon, nor films in Philemon. So, what does the Bible teach us about this apparently vital matter?

God: at work and rest

In the early chapters of Genesis, God is presented to us, in the first place, as a skilled workman. At the end of each day he takes a break and looks at his work. After six days, having finished the job to his own specification, he rests for a whole day and simply enjoys what he's accomplished.

The Bible goes on to teach that the Lord did his work in this way to establish a rhythm for every other work(wo)man who would follow him. In Scripture, the Sabbath is a rest day from work before it becomes a day for religious gathering.

When this is later enshrined in commandment, the people of God are commanded to "do their work" and to "rest". In **Exodus 23 v 12** and **31 v 17** the word "refreshed" is used of both man and God in this connection. It's a word connected to the Hebrew word for "breath" and conveys the idea of getting your breath and energy back. And, of course, God does this by actively enjoying his finished work. He does not become idle on the Sabbath, but ceases productivity and actively enjoys the fruits of his labour.

Eventually, the New Testament takes this concept and presents salvation to us as an eternal "rest" (**Hebrews 4 v 9**), which includes the principle of actively enjoying the fruits of a work Christ Jesus finished for us by his life, death and resurrection.

One fascinating feature of the creation which the Lord actively enjoyed was its lack of strict utilitarianism. God was amazingly super-utilitarian in his work. He took pleasure in producing a world of extravagant variety, astounding colour, and superb sounds. He didn't have to decorate the peacock nor enable the whale to sing bass. Leland Ryken calls it "creative prodigality". The verdict on the Garden of Eden was "pleasant to the sight and good for food" (**Genesis 2 v 9**). Jesus' reflections on the way God clothed the lilies is another example of the principle. Hence, the expressions: "Would you look at that!" or "Have a bite of this!" Josef Pieper says: "The soul of leisure lies in celebration".

What is the connection with leisure? Work is blessing the world with our productivity. Leisure is the celebratory enjoyment of that world for the sake of pleasure and with the core purpose of being refreshed and recreated. Being thus refreshed we can re-enter our world to do some more producing.

As we think about the rest of the Bible we can reflect on:

★ Pleasure in God and his world as a vital human activity (**Psalm 19 v 1; 27 v 4**).

★ Solomon engaged in leisure extensively. His activity was apparently legitimate for a man of God even though on its own it cannot satisfy the human spirit (**Ecclesiastes 2 v 24-26; 3 v 11-13; 5 v 18-19**).

★ Jesus came eating and drinking, just like a happy bridegroom (**John 2 v 1-11**); and he made sure that taking a break (even from evangelism) for fishing, fellowship and feasting was a regular occurrence in the ministry team.

So, Ryken says: "The Biblical principle of rest provides a space within which leisure can occur".[3]

Just do it
Leisure, therefore, must be pursued entirely for its own inbuilt enjoyment. Its value lies in its disconnection from the world of productivity, deadlines, and task-centred goals. There's a tendency in our work-dominated culture to approach leisure as an extension to work. "If I'm to be a good manager, I've got to spend these three grim hours a week down at the gym!" In some circum-

stances a man's leisure might be more important to his personal wellbeing than his job. The school caretaker who plays cello in the local symphony orchestra may well be working to fund his music, and who would blame him as long as he swept the school to the glory of God?

We must not easily swallow the opinion that there's too much leisure in our culture. Staffan Linder in his book *The Harried Leisure Class* argues that as our lifestyle has become more affluent and therefore more demanding, we face a crisis in time available for non-pressurised leisure. E.F. Schumacher says: "The amount of genuine leisure available in a society is generally in inverse proportion to the amount of labour-saving machinery it employs".[4]

I would suggest that we need to "just do it", but with the emphasis on the "do". Much of our available leisure time is spent passively engaging with the television. The biblical principle is the "active" enjoyment of a finished work. The Christian man needs to have a leisure activity which can be enjoyed simply for its own sake. It must be something that will absorb his mind and heart into an enjoyable world away from his productive responsibilities.

There are a vast number of leisure pursuits that are available to us. I'm not going to get into the question of which are more "Christian" than others. Soccer and calligraphy are quite different, but because the Bible was written by calligraphers doesn't make soccer less spiritual as a leisure activity! Of course, there are some activities that are unedifying and incompatible with a godly heart. But, each man must consider his gifts, his interests, passions and abilities, and just get on with his hobby or sport with all his heart. Let him be lost in it for those few blessed hours a week. He will come back to his wife and family (if he has them), back to his work responsibilities and back to his church, refreshed. This will be especially true if, in the course of his leisure, he has enjoyed community, engaged with his kids, strengthened his body, sharpened his mind and beaten the opposition!

Of course, there are God-given limits to this whole matter. Leisure has a unique power to capture the heart of a man idolatrously. Many a man has bowed down before the golf driver or the fishing rod, and neglected his other key responsibilities. He may even have spent a disproportionate amount of money on this good thing. A good thing becomes a bad thing when it harms other more important things (like a wife).

I remember to my shame a Saturday morning in Buckinghamshire. My small daughter (third child after two sons) fell in the kitchen and wounded her temple deeply enough to require stitches. My darling wife rushed to the emergency room with said daughter and sons ... alone. The accident occurred too near kick-off time in the Wycombe & District Football league and her husband "needed" to catch the bus to the match in which he was playing inside right. A touch idolatrous perhaps!

Back to George

So, the Rev. Strong should indulge his passion for squash with all his heart. It strengthens his body, relaxes away his tensions, sends him home glowing with pleasure (well, tired anyway), teaches him to win graciously and lose magnanimously. The more it absorbs him and the greater the pleasure it gives him, the more it partakes of the principle of "rest". It gives him the joy of being with other blokes and enjoying their friendship while trying to beat the pants off them. He doesn't need to justify it on the grounds that it enables him to evangelise the lost or prepare better sermons. He just needs to do it because he absolutely loves it— Just do it, George!

DISCUSS

Q1. Do you feel guilty about your leisure pursuits? Why? Where does leisure fit in your understanding of the role of a godly man?

Q2. What kind of things do you enjoy doing most? Are you developing the kind of leisure involvement that refreshes and recreates you?

Q3. Write down what leisure activities you actually do at the moment. How does each benefit you, and how can they be improved to maximise their benefit in your life?

Further reading

Leland Ryken. *Work and Leisure In Christian Perspective.* (Wipf and Stock Publishers. May 2002)

Josef Pieper. *Only the Lover Sings.* (Ignatius Press 1990)

John Piper. *The Pleasures of God.* (Mentor. 2002)

References

[1] Charter for Leisure, World Leisure Board of Directors, July 2000. World Leisure and Recreation Association.

[2] Leland Ryken. *Work and Leisure In Christian Perspective.* (Wipf and Stock Publishers. May 2002) p 13

[3] *ibid.* p 187

[4] E.F. Schumacher. *Good Work* (New York Harper Row, 1979) p 2

Contributors

Richard Coekin is married to Sian (a doctor) and they have five children. He is a pastor of congregations in Wimbledon and Mayfair. He is also involved in teaching the Bible to workers in London and in the 9:38 ministry-training initiative. Richard is chairman of the organising committee for the London Men's Convention.

Phillip Jensen was chaplain at the University of New South Wales for many years and is now dean of St. Andrews Cathedral, Sydney. He is a well-known speaker at conferences in Australia, England and the USA.

John Benton taught mathematics in a state school before becoming pastor of Chertsey Street Baptist Church, Guildford, UK where he has been for the last 20 years. John has published a number of books and commentaries and edits the newspaper *Evangelicals Now*. He is married to Anne and has four children.

Vaughan Roberts has been on the staff of St Ebbe's Church, Oxford, UK since 1991, where he is now rector. He is involved in 9:38, encouraging younger people to consider the possibility of long-term gospel ministry. In his free time he plays cricket, tennis and golf.

David Jackman is a well-known Bible teacher and preacher. Formerly senior minister of Above Bar Church, Southampton, he is now president of the Proclamation Trust. He has been married to Heather for 30 years. They have a grown-up son and daughter.

Tim Chester is a church planter with The Crowded House and the director of the Northern Training Institute. He's the author of *You Can Change* (IVP) and *Captured By A Better Vision: Living Porn Free* (IVP). He is married to Helen and has two teenage daughters.

Trevor Archer has been married to Valerie for 30 years and they have a grown-up daughter and three sons. Trevor worked in the building industry for 20 years, before becoming the pastor of Chessington Evangelical Church. He is now Director of Training for the Federation of independent Evangelical Churches (FIEC) in the UK.

Hugh Palmer is the rector of All Souls Church, Langham Place in London. He is married to Clare and is a lifelong supporter of Brighton & Hove Albion Football Club.

Tim Thornborough worked as a painter, dancer, social worker and journalist before settling on being a publisher. He is the editorial director of the Good Book Company, is married to Kathy, and has three daughters.

Rico Tice has been curate with responsibility for evangelism at All Souls, Langham place, since 1994, and is the founder of the "Christianity Explored" evangelistic course. Prior to ordination, he worked in training and development at Hewlett Packard. A former captain of the Bristol University rugby team, his hobbies include reading and golf. Rico is married to Lucy and has a young son.

William Taylor is rector of St Helen's Bishopsgate in the City of London. William is married to Janet and they have three children—Emily, Digby and Archie. Before being ordained, William spent five years as an officer in the British Army. He is a keen fly fisherman and enjoys rural pursuits.

John Tindall worked in a bank before training as a Methodist minister. He is now associate pastor at Monyhull church in the UK. He is married to Pauline and has three children and seven grandchildren at the last count. In his leisure time he watches old films and plays with his grandchildren.

Man of God

The Good Book Guide to biblical manhood

man of God

This set of Bible studies aims to unpack the answers the Bible gives to the question of identity that men face today. We will learn our God-given role in creation, how that has been ruined by the fall, and we will discover how we can start to be restored through the man above all men—Jesus Christ. Some things that emerge will be controversial in our culture, even in some of our churches. This course doesn't set out to be politically correct but faithful to God's counter-cultural word.

Suitable for groups or individuals, this guide covers all the major Bible teaching specific to men. Set within the big picture of God's redemption of sinners through Jesus Christ, the heart-felt aim of the authors is that 21st-century men will be set free from the slavery of human expectations, and enabled to live purposefully and confidently for Christ as true Men of God.

10 Studies | ISBN: 9781904889977
Published by The Good Book Company

FOR MORE INFORMATION AND TO ORDER
please visit your friendly neighbourhood website:

UK & Europe: www.thegoodbook.co.uk
N America: www.thegoodbook.com
Australia: www.thegoodbook.com.au
New Zealand: www.thegoodbook.co.nz

thegoodbook
COMPANY

At The Good Book Company, we are dedicated to helping Christians and local churches grow. We believe that God's growth process always starts with hearing clearly what he has said to us through his timeless word—the Bible.

Ever since we opened our doors in 1991, we have been striving to produce resources that honour God in the way the Bible is used. We have grown to become an international provider of user-friendly resources to the Christian community, with believers of all backgrounds and denominations using our Bible studies, books, evangelistic resources, DVD-based courses and training events.

We want to equip ordinary Christians to live for Christ day-by-day, and churches to grow in their knowledge of God, their love for one another, and the effectiveness of their outreach. Call us for a discussion of your needs or visit one of our local websites for more information on the resources and services we provide.

UK & Europe: www.thegoodbook.co.uk
N America: www.thegoodbook.com
Australia: www.thegoodbook.com.au
New Zealand: www.thegoodbook.co.nz

UK & Europe: 0333 123 0880
N America: 866 244 2165
Australia: (02) 6100 4211
New Zealand (+64) 3 343 1990